Design in Airline Travel Posters
1920–1970

Design in Airline Travel Posters 1920–1970

A Semiology and Sociocultural History

David Scott

ANTHEM PRESS

Anthem Press
An imprint of Wimbledon Publishing Company
www.anthempress.com

This edition first published in UK and USA 2022
by ANTHEM PRESS
75–76 Blackfriars Road, London SE1 8HA, UK
or PO Box 9779, London SW19 7ZG, UK
and
244 Madison Ave #116, New York, NY 10016, USA

First published in the UK and USA by Anthem Press in 2021

British Library Cataloguing-in-Publication Data
A catalogue record for this book is available from the British Library.

Library of Congress Control Number: 2020952788

ISBN-13: 978-1-83998-534-8 (Pbk)
ISBN-10: 1-83998-534-8 (Pbk)

This title is also available as an e-book.

For Peter Spearritt,
friend, colleague and inspirational adviser in this project.

CONTENTS

FIGURES

INTRODUCTION

The field of poster studies is a vast one, but it is surprising how little work has been done to date on the fundamental structures – semiotic and semantic – that underpin the visual messages posters produce. Most studies of posters focus on their history (Müller-Brockman & Yoshikawa, 1971; Franciscono, 1987) – very often under the time-worn rubric 'The Golden Age of …' or equivalent periodic markers (Peignot, 1988; Morris, 1989), on specific themes – politics (Gervereau, 1991, 2000; Guillemain, 1991; Weill, 1995), travel (Weill, 1994), sport (Castiglioni, 1986; Durry, 1988), urban life (Moles, 1970), cinema – or on their status as collectable items. Although such approaches are undoubtedly valid, they hardly account for the specificity of the poster's appeal or for the complex semiotic and cultural issues poster art raises. Similarly, though there are a few books devoted to the study of advertising in aviation and air travel in national contexts (Purvis, 1992; Smit, Wunderlinck & Hooland, 1994; Scudiero, Cirulli & Cremoncini, 2002; Woodley, 2004; Cruddas, 2008), to date no book has taken a broader approach to both the form and the content, the medium and the message, of air travel posters. This book sets out to tackle these latter issues since they are fundamental both to the deeper significance and to the wider appeal of the poster as a cultural form, and to an understanding of air travel.

Since posters are cultural signs, to understand better how they work and the value attached to them even after their commercial or political message has been communicated, it is useful to analyse them in terms of both their sociocultural history and their semiological structure. The status of the poster as sign has to date been analysed in depth by Fresnault-Deruelle (1989, 1997) and Scott (2010), while its status as a social and cultural document has been extensively explored by Moles (1970), Spearritt (1990) and others. An illuminating survey of the social history of air travel has moreover been provided by Hudson and Pettifer (1979) and of the role of airline travel in tourism in Australia by Davidson and Spearritt (2010: chapter 10). What my book sets out to do is to combine these two approaches in such a way as to enhance the viewer/reader's understanding of both the cultural and the semiological aspects of the poster and to show how the interaction of these aspects produces the specific quality of its messages.

Although posters are essentially word/image constructs, little attention has in fact been paid to this fundamental aspect of their semiological structure. While Roland Barthes (1964) and other structuralist semioticians of the 1960s and 1970s – in France in particular – have made inroads into what is at stake in the poster's word/image structure, only Scott (2010) to date has pursued the implications of this for the rhetoric of persuasion that is activated by the poster in fulfilling its dual function as provider of information and agent of seduction. For the poster, from the start of the twentieth century, has established a conventional repertory of textual/visual motifs that it has applied across a wide range of communicative functions – political, commercial and artistic. The way these motifs are structured is worth analysing since it reveals much about the way cultural messages are constructed and the way the poster is able to promote both a specific, product-centred message and aesthetic pleasure through a multiplicity of connotations.

Since the range and number of posters produced in the twentieth century are vast, this study will focus on pursuing the vital word/image, semiotic/cultural aspects specific to the poster form in the context of airline travel. This focus has been selected for the following reasons:

1. There is a substantial corpus of airline posters from the development of commercial airlines in the 1920s right through to the end of the century.
2. This corpus comprehensively exhibits the features that characterize the rhetoric of persuasion intrinsic to the poster in the modern world and the way these strategies are modified in the light of changing times, fashions and circumstances.
3. Airline posters offer one of the best contexts in which to examine the development of logo or marque as a key element in commercial brand promotion.
4. As a modern and dynamic means of transport, airline travel has necessitated, in the development of its promotional material, interaction of informative and fantasy components. This is reflected in the way the airline poster balances verifiable information (time, itinerary, destination) and fantasy investment (speed, glamour, exoticism).
5. The complex conceptual issues raised by rapid, long-distance air travel and the concomitant negotiation of different cultures and destinations within a short time period have offered a challenge that has brought the best out of some poster artists (Games, Henrion, Lee-Elliot), leading them to produce airline travel images that are exemplary not only in their period glamour and nostalgia but also in their graphic style's functional efficiency.

The focus of this project will be further narrowed by discussion of airline posters per se rather than by airline advertising in general. So the many newspaper, magazine or brochure advertisements put out by airline companies will only incidentally figure in it. This is because the message function of the poster is different from that of the magazine ad or brochure, in particular in that the latter two types usually contain considerable segments of text in small print. This textual material requires time and attention with the effect that the viewer of the advertisement becomes a reader, being required momentarily to devote his or her attention exclusively to the textual component, whereas in the poster proper the textual message is never viewed in isolation from its image matrix. This book is therefore a study of the *poster as poster* as much as of airline promotional imagery and looks at the latter in terms of the former. As it happens, the themes that dominate in airline advertising, as suggested above, are particularly appropriate to treatment in the rapid, graphic shorthand that is the hallmark of the poster.

Since it is the poster format and functions that constitute the primary focus of this study, these rather than more specific angles – individual themes such as airlines, aircraft, itineraries and periods – will constitute the main thrust of the enquiry. Naturally the themes just mentioned will figure prominently in our discussion of poster design and content, but our main concern will be with how the various themes and subjects articulated in airline posters are shaped and motivated by the poster format itself and what it tells us about the way commercial messages are constructed. And here the main 'themes', those that in effect provide the basis of the chapter headings of this study, reflect both the motivating impulses – destinations and itineraries, glamour and sex appeal, democratizing the skies – and the semiological structures – reading strategies, framing devices and indexical motifs – that shape the fundamental airline poster messages.

The combined treatment of semiological and semantic or ideological elements of the airline poster reflects the author's fundamental commitment in this book to examining the dual implications of poster communication, which is constituted by both message structure and message content. So in what follows, succinct outlines of the general principles operative in posters as communicative structures will be accompanied by a sociocultural analysis of the poster message's essential content. The latter aspect of the subject area, not least in the light of the chronological span of half a century (1920–70) to which this project has restricted itself, is of course potentially unlimited, but this study will attempt nevertheless to restrain itself to the most salient points, points which will in all instances be substantiated by the poster material reproduced in evidence. Naturally the latter will in part be a function of selection – governed in part by the author's particular preferences or proclivities – but the dominant criteria for selection of posters will be the efficiency with which they unite function and fantasy, and express the relationship between denotation and connotation, factual accuracy and desire. Posters will be grouped precisely according to the way in which certain structures and motifs become conventionalized, setting up a repertory of strategies repeatedly articulated in airline advertisement. So each of this book's successive chapters will be built round a corpus of cognate poster images with the aim of foregrounding a visual repertory that substantiates the structural or thematic generalizations put forward in the body of the text. The aim of this approach will also be to show how, in general, the most successful posters are also the most beautiful, beauty in the poster being a function of the optimal coordination of the essential graphic and thematic elements that constitute it.

This latter criterion – that of the *aesthetic* efficiency of the poster image – also plays a governing role in the chronological focus of this study, with its emphasis on the 1920–70 period. This was a time when the commercial poster in the West (which includes for these purposes Australasia) – in particular in the 1920s, 1930s and 1940s – was establishing a new level of graphic and thematic sophistication, drawing on the lessons of Futurism, Cubism and Art Deco, as well as on the massive expansion of consumer culture. The use of colour lithography and to a lesser extent photo-montage has provided the means of producing images that combined spectacular visual appeal with clarity and legibility, in a symbiosis that has scarcely been rivalled since. As it happens, the advent of modern colour photography and mass televisual information coincided with both the decline of the airline poster and the increased democratization of airline travel, as the jet age and the intense commercial competition of the 1960s ushered in a very different approach to airline promotion. This change will be the subject of this study's concluding chapter.

Airline travel posters, like other Western representations of exotic destinations or objects of desire, are of course guilty of the essentialism that seems unavoidable when one culture attempts to represent another, especially for commercial purposes. From a postcolonial perspective, a number of the posters examined in this book might in strict terms be judged ideologically problematic as they in various ways glamorize, caricature, falsify or misrepresent aspects of the target culture. They might by the same token be judged guilty of orientalism as defined by Edward Said in his influential book of that title (1979), that is, of the representation of another culture better to possess, exploit or dominate it in commercial, political or other ideological terms. The main Western airlines whose posters are studied here (Imperial Airways/BOAC; Air Orient/Air France; KLM) were all, as the names of some of them suggest, founded as part of an imperialist project whereby the rapid movement of people, post, goods and other commercial elements would strengthen the power and influence of Western nations in other parts of the world, in particular Africa and the Middle and Far East. In this way, Western modes of representation become part of the imperialist strategy, strengthening its persuasiveness by the very attractiveness of the propaganda it produced. So the more aesthetically pleasing and functional of the posters examined may by that very token make them more prone to cultural essentialism. However, if a deeper understanding of the way one culture inevitably (mis-)represents another is to be had, the processes involved have to be analysed, if not totally objectively (this would be impossible) then at least from a clearly stated bias. It is not the aim of the author of this book to pass moral judgement on the material examined, but to show as fully as possible the semiotic and cultural issues at stake in touristic representation. In the process a degree of tolerance and humour is presupposed on the part of readers, many of whom, in the twenty-first century, will, it is hoped, be themselves indigenous to the cultures formerly represented or misrepresented in the posters of the predominantly Western airlines focused on here. A chapter of the book is in any case devoted to the question of the representation of indigenous people in airline posters of the colonial period.

It is worth noting here finally that the decline of the airline poster coincides with the demise of colonial empires (in particular those of Britain and France). Colonies in Africa, in particular, were gaining independence (in theory if not necessarily in practice) in the late 1950s and 1960s, that is, at the moment when jet-powered civil aircraft were beginning to become the norm in airline travel. The date of 1970, marking more or less exactly half a century of innovatory travel poster design (1920–70), is thus chosen as the limit of the period of study of this book. As Chapter 1 will argue, in the postcolonial, post piston engine age, cultural parameters markedly change, with the balance between information and fantasy that characterized the posters of the earlier period losing its magical spell as advertising more generally adapts to a more homogenized, global style of product marketing.

Chapter 1

FACT AND FANTASY: READING AND MISREADING THE POSTER IMAGE

This chapter centres on the airline poster image's double status: objective information *and* subjective fantasy or desire. The richness of airline posters in the early modern age of graphic reproduction (1920–50, with 1950–70 marking a transition period) is invariably a function of this double agenda. For the poster's aim is to portray an image that elicits from the viewer intense identification through both its formal structure and its ostensible content. In poster art, visual strategies are therefore developed to maximize viewer identification on both a rational *and* a fantasy level. Sometimes it is the appeal of the graphic image that fulfils desire while the textual component supplies the objective information. At other times, the textual message itself becomes as much a seductive agent as the image – as in those memorable and enticing slogans developed by many airline companies from the 1940s. Alternatively, in the most successful posters, it is the indissoluble combination of the two, text and image, that ensnares or enchants the viewer/reader who is invited to bring both textual and visual understanding to bear on the unravelling of the poster message. In this way the most persuasive posters mobilize a rhetoric of image-text that the very act of apprehension persuades the receiver to enter into, inviting them to enjoy the poster's creation of meaning as an enticing textual/visual *game* (see Scott, 2010).

It is the desire or fantasy aspect of the image that normally comes across as strongest in the travel poster. But there is always a risk attached to it. Whereas the objective, factual aspect of the poster information can be verified and is rarely problematic, the desire element is very much open to interpretation. The poster designer of course aims to control that interpretation (see Scott, 2010) so that it is correctly grasped. If he or she fails, the outcome can be disastrous, as in those posters in which the real/informational element of the poster fails to temper and control the fantasy element. A striking example of this is provided by one in a series of Australian Airlines posters of 1990, examined below, in which the real destination of the airline, though visually present, is upstaged or falsified by an attendant erotic scenario that was so misread by its intended audience that the poster had to be quickly withdrawn. This and other instructive successes and failures of *semiosis* or meaning-construction in the airline poster will be examined in some detail in this chapter as they tell us much about the way desire has as far as possible to be controlled by the image designer in the light of the poster's primary message.

Where, on the other hand, a poster designer fully integrates the factual/ objective with the fantasy/desire elements, the perfect poster results. Masters such as F. H. K. Henrion, Tom Eckersley and Abram Games (for BOAC) and Perceval, Badia Vilato and Roger de Valério (for Air France) in the 1940s, 1950s and 1960s (the height of the poster's early modern development) managed, as I shall show, sometimes through a cunning use of the airline logo (itself both a mythical and a factual sign), to achieve this unity, which makes their posters exemplary, even today. There can be little doubt that the peculiar ability of the lithographic poster to harmonize text and image (in a way that photographic posters seldom do) was instrumental in effecting this persuasive unity of objective truth and fantasy desire.

Since no text or image is ever absolutely unambiguous in its message or proposition, the question of a correct or incorrect reading can never be fully resolved. On the whole, textual messages in prose are less ambiguous since they are semantically highly structured following fixed conventions of grammar and syntax. The visual image, on the other hand, is both more immediately sensuous in its appeal and less fixed in its denotative meaning, with connotations – consciously or unconsciously intended – creeping into both the production and reception of meaning within it. This is of course part of the richness of the visual image and one of the reasons for its massive exploitation in commercial advertising and in visual culture generally. But the expressive potential of the image brings with it the risk of misinterpretation whereby a meaning or connotation different from – or even opposite to – the one intended by the image-producer is adduced by the image-receiver. Commercial companies invest heavily in market research to ensure that their logos, trademarks or other visual identifiers are received by a broad public in the manner intended. They do this since misinterpretation can have disastrous consequences for the success of the product or service being advertised (see Scott, 2010: 30).

A striking example of just such a misinterpretation is provided by the Australian Airlines poster by Scanlon of 1990, just mentioned, one of a series promoting flights to the Gold Coast and other tourist regions in Queensland and New South Wales (Figure 1.1). The poster in question is an almost caricatural demonstration of the proposition defended in this chapter that the airline poster is doubly motivated – both to provide information and to stimulate desire. Here this dichotomy is crudely illustrated by the division of the poster

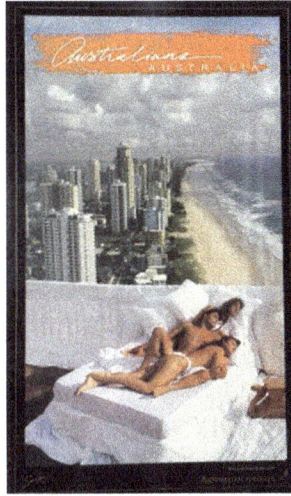

Figure 1.1 Australian Airlines Gold Coast, Scanlon, 1990

into two photographic images: the top one, intended to be factual, shows an aerial view of the high-rise hotel and apartment buildings that line the shores of the Gold Coast region, the destination of the Australian Airlines flight; the bottom image shows a balcony scene in which a naked and muscular male is indulging in sexual foreplay with two beautifully toned and naked women. The fantasy status of this part of the image is indicated by the immaculate whiteness of the sheets in which the trio disport themselves, with even the balcony rails being improbably swathed in white drapery, the photogenic beauty of the participants and the unlikely projection of such activity in broad daylight on a balcony overlooking a banal view. The intended meaning of the scenario, aimed at the white, heterosexual Australian male, is that on the Gold Coast the latter can freely fulfil his erotic fantasies.

To say that this poster was not well received by its public, intended or unintended, would be an understatement. It was immediately withdrawn since, among other reasons, it was seen to promote, in the age of AIDS, an image of promiscuous and unsafe sex. But apart from the crudeness of the poster's image structure and the lack of subtlety in its appeal to the viewer's desires, it represents a more general failure in semiotic terms in that it does not seem to reflect coherent thinking about either of the images exploited or the way they are juxtaposed. The 'factual' image, showing a view of Gold Coast urbanization, is unglamorous enough to suggest that it is appealing to a wide range of potential customers for such seaside apartments, ranging from prosperous middle-class families to retirement couples. But this intention sits uneasily with the colour magazine fantasy of the sex scene which is likely to appeal to a narrower band of potential customers, for whom the image of high-rise building in the background would have negligible appeal. Overall, then, the poster, setting aside its moral ambiguity, is both an artistic and a semiotic failure, delivering neither on the level of subtle, erotic or sensuous desire nor on the level of meaning-creation. For in the process of *semiosis* or meaning-creation in the poster, an intended message would normally be enhanced, not problematized, by alluring sensuous overtones: at the same time, the fantasy or game element of the image would be enriched and not be jeopardized by the poster's essential message. The lesson the Australian Airlines poster provides is that an inability to control the message of the constituent images and effectively to coordinate their interaction will result in failure on both counts – information and fantasy.

By contrast, a BOAC poster of 1959 (Figure 1.2) advertising flights to South America shows how the dual requirements of information and fantasy can be satisfied within one carefully conceived framework and, in the process, a seductive image created. This poster is one in a long line of travel images promoting the idea of 'Flying down to Rio', which, since the 1933 Hollywood movie of that name, confirmed Rio in the public imagination as one of the most glamorous and exotic destinations in the world. Rio de Janeiro, the capital of Brazil until 1960 when the seat of government moved to the new and purpose-built city of Brasilia, was then, as it still is today, the principal international airport of Brazil, indeed of South America; even the larger and commercially more important Brazilian city of São Paulo takes second place as an international airline hub. But this objective significance of Rio as a principal air hub is also strengthened massively in the public imagination by the glamour associated with the city, a glamour based on its stupendous geographical setting, with its Atlantic beaches, on its spectacular Sugarloaf mountain and interconnecting bays and on its reputation as a city of exotic festivity, entertainment and romance, centred not least on its famous carnival.

From the start, therefore, Rio has more going for it than the Australian Gold Coast shown in the Australian Airlines ad, this beach-side city being a relative upstart in potential glamour destinations, its rise to prominence as a tourist paradise dating only from the 1960s when the surfing craze was reaching new heights in Queensland and New South Wales. But the BOAC Rio poster succeeds where the Australian Airlines one fails in that it manages seamlessly in one unified yet striking image to combine an appeal to both the real and the imaginary potential of Rio as a destination. It does this by adopting three strategies in relation to its graphic presentation. One, by choosing to display all information, textual or visual, against the same black background, the poster immediately places all aspects of its proposed message *on the same*

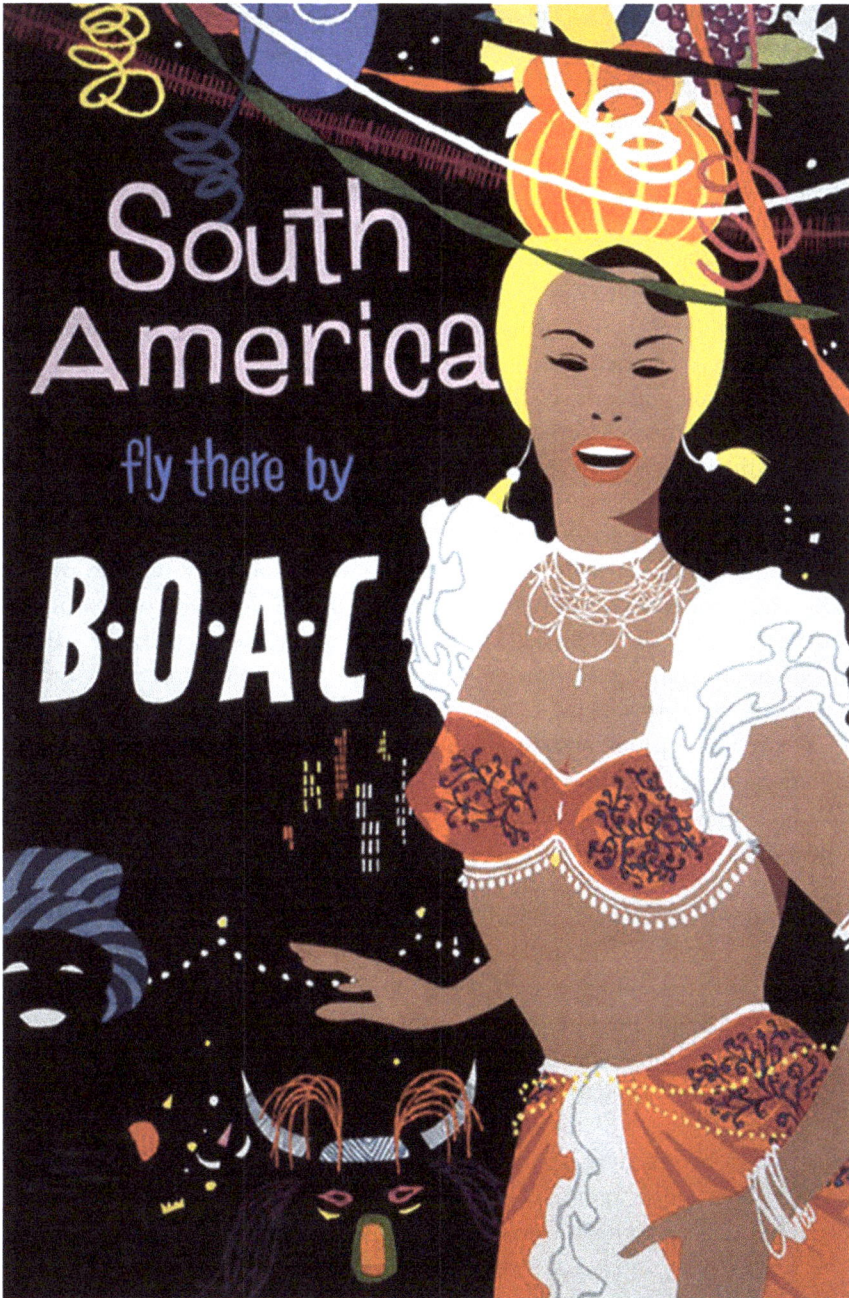

Figure 1.2 South America Fly there by BOAC, 1959

level. Factual information – name of airline, place of destination – stands out as spectacular visual motifs against the exotic, night-time background in the same way that the samba dancer surges from the tropical night to personify the imagined erotic pleasures of Rio. Second, this crucial design decision has the positive effect of enabling the *textual* as well as the visual elements of the scene to be read on a primary level, offering therefore no jarring change of medium or register which, as we saw in the Australian Gold Coast poster, tends to fragment or problematize rather than unify the proposed message. So, whereas the Gold Coast poster crudely superimposes in a clumsy tautology 'Australia by Australian Airlines' onto the photo of the Gold Coast shoreline, in the Rio poster, the famous BOAC acronym is suspended like a glowing neon sign in the night sky of the Rio setting, in this way becoming itself part of the glamour of the scenario in which it is incorporated. Third, the strobe effect of the bright lights against the unified dark background has the result of seductively drawing the poster viewer's attention to the colours and lights that mark out the textual as well as the visual aspects of the scene, enabling them to be imagined as offering both a real perspective on the city and opening up avenues for erotic reverie. In this way the BOAC acronym, shining in the darkness, operates as a magical agent bringing about the possibility of experiencing the imagined pleasures promised by the Brazilian dancer who sambas towards us in a provocative, Carmen Miranda-like movement.

The ultimate proof perhaps of the BOAC Rio poster's semiotic efficiency is the relative timelessness it achieves, the image still having an appeal today, half a century after its creation. This timelessness is a function of the poster's beauty, by which we mean its perfect coordination of the essential graphic and thematic elements that constitute it: nothing in the image is superfluous, nothing unintentionally ambiguous; there is no element of the image that does not play a necessary role in the creation of the overall effect which is one of glamour and sensual appeal. And yet the latter, unlike the overdetermined, erotic scenario proposed by the Australian Airlines poster, is not allowed to become overdominant or separate from the central, informational message of the poster. All is unified in a joyous celebration of the real possibility of experiencing the pleasures of the indicated destination. Of course, these pleasures may in part be imaginary, but then the successful poster is always to a certain degree the proposition or articulation of a *myth*. The trick is to make the myth plausible, to make it as universally acceptable as possible, to make it pleasurable even as it reminds the viewer that of course it is in part an illusion, an effect like that of strobe lights on a darkened dance floor or neon signs in the tropical night.

The mythical potential of the airline travel poster is one that graphic artists and sales managers seem to have grasped from the inception of national airlines

Figure 1.3 Air France (seahorse or *hypocampe* logo), Roger de Valério, 1935

and their concomitant promotion in the 1920s. It is evident not only in the fantasy content of most poster themes – the colourful destination, the exotic woman, the magical power of the airline and aircraft and the global reach of both – but also in the trademark or logo – most often a real or mythical animal or bird – around which airline companies forged their identity and which they used to promote their standing on a national and international level. So the Air France (formerly Air Orient) *hypocampe* (Figure 1.3) and the BOAC (formerly Imperial Airways) *Speedbird* (Figure 1.4) represented for over 50 years two of the world's leading airlines (both logos date from 1932), while the Qantas kangaroo (1920, Figure 1.5) and Lufthansa crane (1950s, Figure 1.6), dating from the 1920s, go back even further. Not surprisingly some of the earliest mythical incarnations of airline travel are based on classical European mythic archetypes – Icarus (Figure 1.7), Pegasus, mythical birds (the American Airlines eagle) – or on more recently instituted and conventionalized female national deities – Marianne (Figure 1.8) and Italia (Figure 1.9). Since airline logos represent in a concentrated form the essence of national carriers' commercial ideology and are systematically used in their airline posters as a focus of promotional strategies, it is worth looking at their inception and elaboration in more detail (for a full account, see Scott, 2010: Chapter 2).

Classical deities, most often female, were still a standard national identity sign for many European countries at the start of the twentieth century (see Scott, 1995). Helvetia, Germania, Britannia and even Hibernia regularly appeared on definitive postage stamps and coinage, as did the more recently

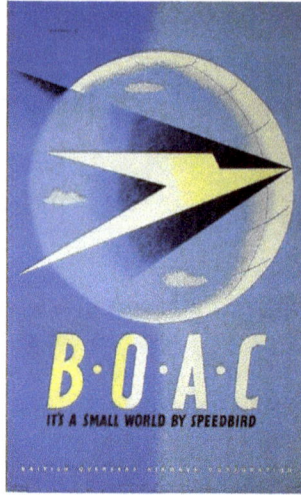

Figure 1.4 It's a small world by Speedbird Fly BOAC, Tom Eckersley, 1947

Figure 1.5 Qantas Empire Airways (winged kangaroo logo), 1930s

instituted French national icon, Marianne, in her various guises (Liberty, the Sower) (see Scott 2002). However, after an initial appearance on some pro-motional posters (Figures 1.8 and 1.9), they tended, like Icarus (Figure 1.7), to fall from grace. In the case of the latter, this was for obvious reasons: who would choose a mythical figure whose wings fell off when he flew too high, to

Figure 1.6 Lufthansa (crane logo), 1950s

Figure 1.7 Deutsche Lufthansa (Icarus), 1936

promote an airline? On the other hand, the early demise of Italia (replaced later on Alitalia aircraft by a tail configuration using the colours of the Italian flag in a harder-edged and more dynamic configuration) and Marianne was in part a reflection of national airlines' wish to promote a new and distinctive aspect of their profile in their propaganda material. So, the introduction in

Figure 1.8 Locomotion aérienne (Marianne), Charles Fouqueret, 1919

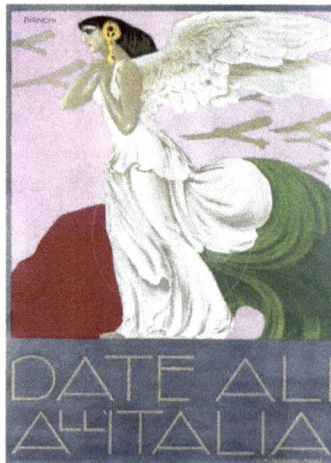

Figure 1.9 Date Ali All'Italia, Alberto Bianchi, 1920s

1932 of such crucial logos as Imperial Airways/BOAC's Speedbird and Air Orient/Air France's seahorse or *hypocampe* was conceived to express the more specific and distinctive attributes of the airline – speed, strength, long-distance capability – that would enhance its identity and competitiveness in the modern world. The point is made in allegorical terms by one of the best-known and

successful early Air France posters (1935, Figure 1.3) in which the French deity
of flight is seen to rise up from the nose of one of the airline's modern aircraft and to affix against the globe the recently instituted Air France seahorse
logo. Thereafter, this female deity never again figured on Air France posters,
whereas the seahorse logo for the rest of the century was widely incorporated
into the airline's livery and promotional material.

The power and mythical prestige of the airline logo perhaps finds its finest
expression in one of the most popular and successful airline posters of all
time, F. H. K. Henrion's *It's a small world by Speedbird*, designed for BOAC in
1947 (Figure 1.10). Selected as one of the best posters of the year, it appeared
in the International Poster Annual of 1948 and has been acknowledged ever
since as an object lesson in effective graphic design. Like the BOAC Rio poster
of 1959, analysed above, its success is based on a masterly coordination of
mythical and actual elements, achieving a synthesis of information and fantasy, accuracy and myth. Like the BOAC Rio poster, it was able to do this by
setting the actual/informational elements of the poster message – BOAC's
international routes marked on a map of the world, the flags of all the countries visited – on the same level as the fantasy elements – the dream of being
whisked skywards by some magic bird and being swiftly and safely delivered
to one of a wide choice of destinations. In the case of the Henrion poster, it is
the Speedbird logo itself that pulls off the conjuring trick as it sweeps up the
longitudinal lines of the globe in its beak and redistributes them in a colourful
display of flags marking the destinations served by BOAC.

What is significant here is the way this magical transformation is commented
on in the graphic terms that are used to pull it off. Henrion makes the real surface of the map of the world contiguous with the visited countries' national
flags, the shift from indexical (map) to iconic sign (flag) being achieved as it
were on the *same surface of representation* with a mere twist of paper. Similarly, the
textual elements of the poster message – *it's a small world by Speedbird* and the
company acronym *B O A C* – are aligned in such a way as to become integral
with the more purely visual constituents of the poster message. So, the bold
italic capitals ***B O A C*** provide the perturbation in the globe's longitudinal
lines that makes possible the transformation of travel distance into destination,
while the slogan *it's a small world by Speedbird* both comments on and reflects the
visual message into which it is seamlessly woven. In this way the poster, the
work of a conjurer in graphic design, succeeds in showing the viewer the way
the message is constructed precisely as it articulates it.

The Henrion poster also, in the process, revitalizes the repertory of
standard visual motifs (globes, airline itineraries, slogans) established in airline
posters over preceding decades, by exploiting their *metaphorical* potential, that
is, by fully integrating textual and visual motifs in such a way that they express

Figure 1.10 It's a small world by Speedbird BOAC, F. H. K. Henrion, 1947

both real and mythical (metaphorical) possibilities. This refined approach will in the following decade be widely employed by airline poster artists from Abram Games and Beverly Pick for BOAC to Plaquet and Badia Vilato for Air France. So, posters by Pick (Figure 1.11) and Vilato (Figure 1.12) show how such standard visual motifs as globe, sky, directional indictor (compass or arrow) and, most importantly, company logo and slogans can be incorporated in analogous but distinctive ways to create compelling messages. In Pick's poster of 1948, the proposition that *it's a smaller world by Speedbird* is incontrovertibly asserted by the comparison of the compact modern globe in red, sent spinning by the passage of the Speedbird logo flying around it, with that of the much larger and sepia-coloured sixteenth-century world of maritime travel behind. Oblivious to the winds and currents that made travel in the age of sailing ships both treacherous and slow, the Speedbird of modern-day air travel arrows straight to its destination. In a similar way, the Badia Vilato Air France poster of three years later (1951, Figure 1.12) shows how the mythical Pegasus, still a configuration of stars in the night sky, is about to be overtaken by a modern Constellation (a Lockheed aircraft of that name) that, bearing the Air France livery, will deliver its passengers swiftly and smoothly to their chosen destination anywhere on the globe (*Dans tous les ciels*). The mythical potential of Pegasus is thus reappropriated by the modern airline whose seahorse logo nevertheless marks its mythical allegiance to the divine powers of classical deities. As with the Henrion poster, those of Pick and Vilato both manage to explore the real and the fantasy dimensions of the airline message on the same level of graphic representation, in this way persuading the viewer to accept and to enjoy form and meaning as indissociable parts of one seductive package.

The mythical power of animal or bird persists, however, as a persuasive motif in a number of airline posters of the 1920s–60s period beyond its specific use in airline logos. The representation of a continent as an animal, for example, can be seen in a BOAC poster of the early 1960s in which the diversity of vast regions and varying cultures merges to form the head of an elephant (Figure 1.13). Playing on the similarity of shape of the African continent with that of the head of its largest animal, the poster designer succeeds in creating a playful but compelling synthesis of the human and zoological, traditional and modern aspects of the destinations served by the BOAC Comet 4 that jets into the picture from the left. A similar strategy was employed by Lucien Boucher in an Air France poster of 1950 (Figure 1.14) in which the wing of Pegasus (on which the Air France seahorse logo is discreetly superimposed) is raised to reveal the matching profile of the continent of South America. As in the BOAC Africa poster, the South American continent's main cities and geographical features are marked out in Boucher's poster, suggesting the

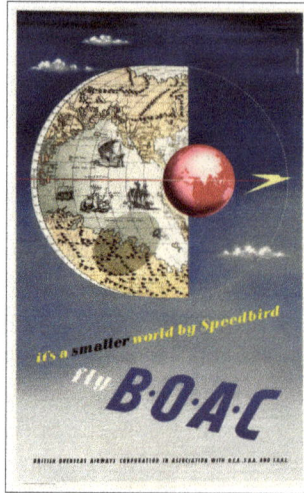

Figure 1.11 It's a smaller world by Speedbird BOAC, Beverley Pick, 1948

Figure 1.12 Air France, Badia Vilato, 1951

potential riches that unfold with the flap of an Air France aircraft's wing. As in the BOAC poster, the aircraft itself, in this case a Lockheed Constellation, is seen flying into the picture from the right, across the south Atlantic Ocean.

The bird's wing, in particular, has established itself in airline posters sufficiently (as it has in other symbolic forms relating to human flight, such as

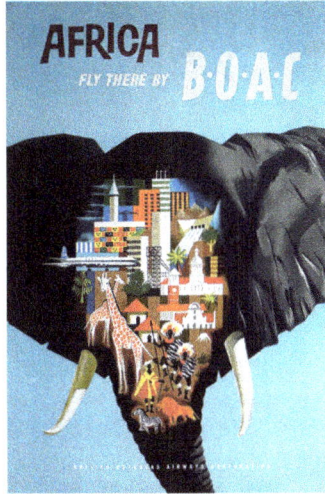

Figure 1.13 Africa Fly there by BOAC, 1960s

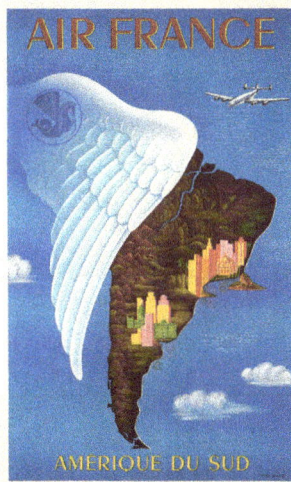

Figure 1.14 Air France Amérique du Sud, Lucien Boucher, 1950

airline or military uniform insignia) for it to become a motif susceptible to articulation in a *visual* syntax that is capable of expressing a persuasive argument. In an SISA poster of the early 1930s, for example (Figure 1.15), we see constructed a visual sentence in which there are four essential components, of which three are visual (or iconic) and one linguistic (or symbolic). Reading

Figure 1.15 SISA (Societa Italiana di Serviza Aeri Trieste), 1930s

Figure 1.16 Air France/Eastern Airlines, Plaquet, 1950

from the bottom left, we see the SISA acronym superimposed on a mythical bird's wing, on which is in turn superimposed a modern Italian tri-motor seaplane, the ensemble flying above a map of Italy on which is marked the route map indicating the airline's operations in the northern part of the country. A similarly complex syntax of visual motifs is coordinated in Plaquet's Air

France poster of 1950 (Figure 1.16) in which a pair of wings linked by rings symbolizing the national flags of France and the United States is superimposed on a globe showing the flight routes of the two airways – Air France and Eastern Airlines – marked out on the four continents that together they serve. A Constellation aircraft crosses the Atlantic confirming the link between a flight on two networks that can be booked using only one ticket. In the process, the poster's simple verbal message 'Air France, Eastern Airlines: deux réseaux, un seul billet' is confirmed in visual terms that together constitute a visually stimulating and persuasive message. In this way, the objective information of the poster, articulated in the linguistic message, is enhanced by the mythical elements whose fascinating visual coordination undoubtedly enhances the persuasive logic of the poster image. The abandonment of this sort of subtle yet complex approach to word/image coordination by airline posters after the 1960s spells the end of that period's conception of air travel.

Chapter 2

PEOPLE, PLACES AND PLANES: DESTINATIONS AND ITINERARIES

Imperial Itineraries

The development from the 1920s of the classic continental or intercontinental itineraries by small but growing airlines was a response in particular to the need to provide rapid transport for both mail and passengers. For the victorious post-World War I European powers (Britain, France and the Netherlands) this meant servicing the routes to their imperial/colonial colonies and dominions as flown by Air Orient (later Air France), Imperial Airways (later BOAC) and KLM (Royal Dutch Airlines), while for American airlines (especially Pan American) it meant covering their sphere of influence with 'Clipper' services to South and Central as well as to North America, using both land and sea planes. At the same time, the growing demand on the part of a wider European and American public in the 1920s and 1930s for travel (business or pleasure-related) to the exotic parts of the world – India, Ceylon, Indonesia and to the colonial dominions in Africa, Australia and New Zealand – resulted in the establishment of a number of world-wide air networks. Very soon European airlines were claiming to travel to 'All six continents', to fly 'Dans tous les ciels' and generally reducing intercontinental travel times to a matter of days rather than weeks.

As a result of this, in the 1930s, the globe or map of the world naturally became a central motif in airline advertising, particularly for European airways. KLM, servicing Dutch interests in the Far East, in particular Indonesia, and in Europe, reminded the public through their posters of the extent and regularity of their flights. So, in a poster of the 1930s (Figure 2.1), a KLM Douglas DC 3 (Dakota) is seen flying above a globe on which are marked KLM routes from Amsterdam across Europe to Cairo, Bagdad, Karachi, Calcutta, Rangoon and Bangkok to the final destination in Batavia (which today we call Jakarta), a journey which in its entirety then took five and a half days, available in both directions twice weekly. A similar approach was taken by KLM to its

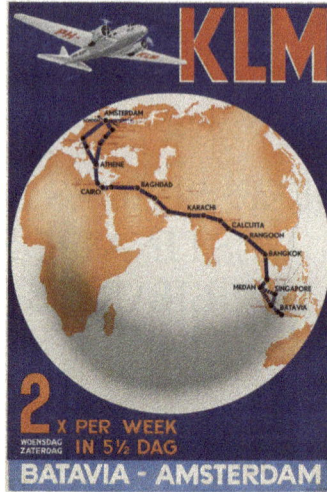

Figure 2.1 KLM Batavia-Amsterdam, Vinci, 1936

European routes (Figure 2.2), which flew from Amsterdam as far south as Milan, especially when, after its launch in 1919, the service established its profile as a major continental airline, with regular flights from, for example, Amsterdam to London initiated as early as 1920. On the other side of the world, Australia's then fledgling airline, Qantas, established in 1920, was similarly using, by the 1930s, an effective combination of maps and signposts to show both its long intercontinental routes (coordinated with those, first, of Imperial Airways and, later, those of BOAC) and its coverage of important destinations in Australia itself. To this purpose, in 1934 the offshoot company Qantas Empire Airlines was formed to coordinate British and Australian airline services in the Far East.

The British, with their imperial routes stretching to the Far East, to Australia as well as to Africa and the West Indies, were masters at promoting their international routes with an imaginative use of maps. The high standard of British cartography and map design, demonstrated most famously by the London Underground railway map by Harry Beck in 1931, was carried over into airline posters of the 1930s, as can be seen in the masterly presentation of Imperial Airways' routes in a poster of 1938 (Figure 2.3). An equally elegant solution to combining aircraft, route and navigational paraphernalia is to be found in an Ala Littoria poster of the same period (Figure 2.4). The inspired British way with airline maps was in evidence again after World War II when BOAC, established in 1939, had replaced Imperial Airways as the chief British overseas carrier. Henrion's 1947 masterpiece 'It's a small world by Speedbird

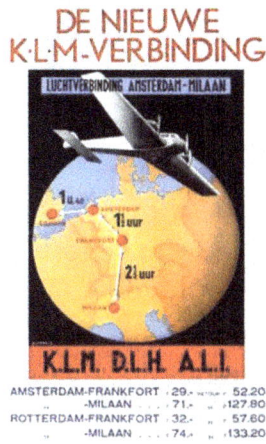

Figure 2.2 De Nieuwe KLM Verbinding (KLM European routes), 1920s

Figure 2.3 Imperial Airways (Empire routes), 1938

BOAC' (Figure 1.10), in which the globe's longitudinal and latitudinal lines are swept up by the beak of the magical Speedbird over a map showing the company's principal routes, has already been analysed in Chapter 1, but the formula he brought to perfection in this poster is also ably amplified by contemporary graphic designers such as Abram Games and Beverley Pick. So, in his

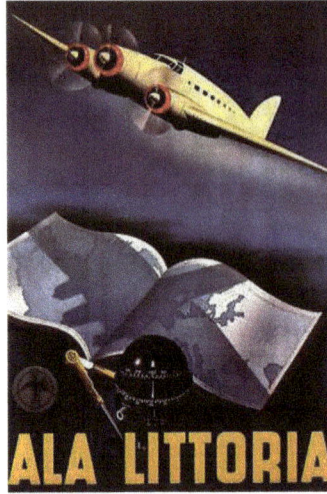

Figure 2.4 Ala Littoria (airline routes), 1938

'Fly the Atlantic' poster (Figure 2.5), Games shows how the seas between Britain and America can be compressed in a flight by Speedbird as if by closing the leaves of an atlas that had been opened at the pages showing the Atlantic Ocean.

Two posters of the early 1950s show the subtle transformation that the onset of jet travel will bring to the representation of routes and itineraries. With the introduction by BOAC in 1952 of the new De Havilland Comet 1, halving flight times on the intercontinental routes, it was no longer necessary to mark on the service's posters the long intercontinental itineraries on the world map or pinpoint the places of stopover, half of which could now be done away with. So in Beverley Pick's 1953 poster 'BOAC flies to all six continents' (Figure 2.6), a globe unmarked by routes is shown to be effortlessly circumnavigated in a sweeping figure of six by the new Comet aircraft, while in another BOAC poster of the same period and the same title (Figure 2.7), Abram Games has merely to point out in vivid colours the six directions BOAC's Speedbird aircraft follow in servicing the continents of the world to express the airline's global range.

As we saw in Chapter 1, Air France posters of the early 1950s followed a similar pattern to those of BOAC in their use of globes or maps (see Badia Vilato's poster of 1951, Figure 1.12), though more often poster artists used by the French airline adopted a more iconic approach to their representation of circumnavigation of the globe. In a 1937 poster (Figure 2.8), N. Gérale shows a Dewoitine aircraft flying out of the sun, on which an outline of the Air France *hypocampe* logo is superimposed, to spread its wings over 14 different

Figure 2.5 Fly the Atlantic by BOAC, Abram Games, 1949

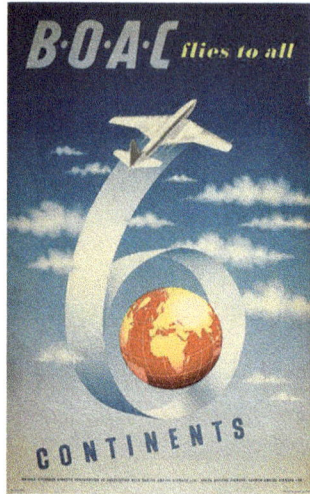

Figure 2.6 BOAC flies to all six continents, Beverley Pick, 1953

Figure 2.7 BOAC flies to all six continents, Abram Games, 1956

world destinations, each of which is marked along the borders of the poster by native types of the countries visited. In a poster of the late 1940s, 'Air France rayonne sur le monde' (Figure 2.9) the *hypocampe* logo and sun motif are again used, this time shining ('rayonant') on the totality of the globe that is being flown by one of the new Lockheed Constellation aircraft, introduced in 1946. A comparison of these two posters is instructive in that it shows how

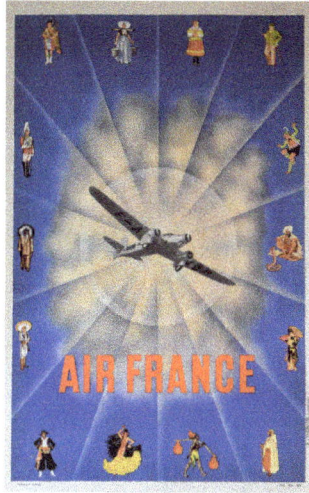

Figure 2.8 Air France autour du monde, N. Gérale, 1937

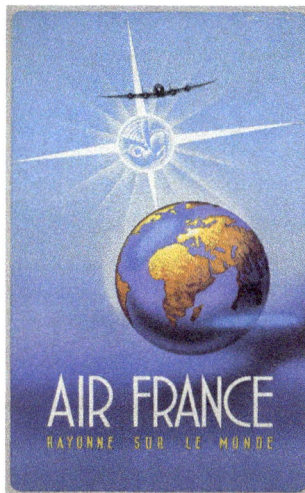

Figure 2.9 Air France rayonne sur le monde, E. Maurus, 1940s

the various iconic motifs selected by the graphic designer – globe, sun, aircraft, airline logo – can be variously assembled to produce subtly different though essentially cognate messages about the company's international services.

Perhaps the ultimate use of the globe as both a focus and a sign of an airline's worldwide range is that shown by an Aeroflot poster of the early 1960s (Figure 2.10). Here, in the age of early space travel, jet aircraft merely

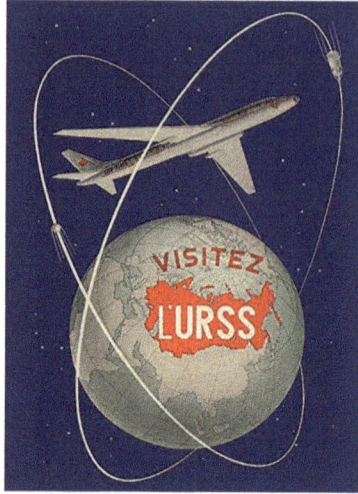

Figure 2.10 Visitez l'URSS Aeroflot, 1960s

revolve in the stratosphere, while the sputniks of the Russian space agency are seen to follow their trajectories beyond the globe, opening up potentially limitless itineraries for travel and exploration. In the light of these vertiginous possibilities, airline posters from the later 1960s largely abandon the map and itinerary approach to air travel and concentrate more on expressing the idea of the latter in terms of ease, convenience and quality of service. So in a KLM poster of the 1950s (Figure 2.11), images of aircraft, globes and itineraries are abandoned in favour of a little still-life in which the colonial pith helmet and an airline brochure incorporating an unmarked map of the world are presented against a background of perspectival lines leading to a vanishing point. A kind of conceptual abstraction of the idea more tangibly expressed in the Air Afrique poster of 1936 (Figure 3.18), analysed in Chapter 3, this poster expresses the idea of travel to the Far East as an effortless undertaking, one following the ticket's brief to the letter and delivering the passenger without mishap – but also without adventure – to his destination.

A similarly abstract configuration of objects assembled to express both the ease and yet the infinite possibilities of travel is expressed in posters of the mid-1950s that use the mobile aircraft entry stairway as the central motif. An Aer Lingus poster adopts this motif expressing the idea that travel to Ireland by air is as simple as ABC or as ascending the gangway into the aircraft. In contrast, the use by Abram Games (Figure 2.12) of the same motif, as has been shown elsewhere (Scott, 2010: 40–41), gives rise to semiotic conceits that are multiple and illuminating; however, at bottom, the message, like that of the

Figure 2.11 KLM Verre Osten (Far East), Guus Melai, 1953

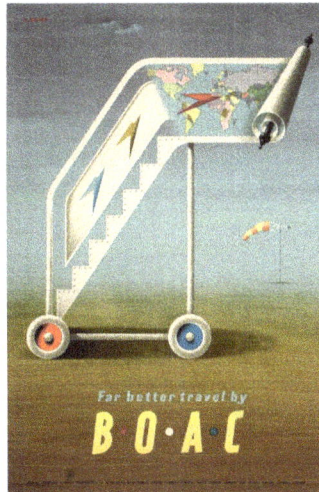

Figure 2.12 Far better travel by BOAC, Abram Games, 1951

Aer Lingus poster, is simple: no need any more for the air traveller to worry about routes, itineraries, stopovers or even the nature of the aircraft; he or she has only to mount the gangway and be transported through the sky or clouds (which form the backdrop to both posters) safely and without incident to the designated destination.

In the light of the above, in the postcolonial age of the 1960s and after, one that coincided with the decline of the airline poster in terms of both graphic quality and impact, it tends to be only the erotic/fantasy element that remains open to development within the advertising image. The rational, practical aspect, in the age of the wide-body jet, is taken for granted, with the necessary information in the twenty-first century being provided online. The one exception until recently was Concorde which (until it was eventually grounded in 2005) still proposed a super-alluring image on the level of both function (halving regular jet travel times) and desire (travel as sign of celebrity). But to appreciate the full impact of this post-1960s simplification in approach to airline promotion through posters, it is necessary to go back and look in further detail at the evolution of that heady mix of fact and fantasy that made airline posters of the pre-jet age such objects of pleasure and fascination.

Aircraft Types

In the early days of scheduled flights, that is, in the 1920s and 1930s, run by national airlines (Air France, Imperial Airways, KLM, Pan Am), passengers were almost as interested in the aircraft as in the destinations to which they would convey them. A majority of the passengers were adult males, many of whom would have throughout their boyhood lived on a diet of popular literature celebrating technological advances, not least in the aeronautical sphere. In response to the passengers' need for information and fantasy identification with the magical craft that would deliver them hundreds or thousands of miles in a matter of hours or days, many airlines produced posters that, like pull-out sections in 1950s schoolboy magazines or comics, showed cross sections of the aircraft currently in use, showing in particular the disposition of the interior arrangements and the services provided. Seaplanes, in particular, with their multiple decks, promenade spaces and often separate pilot and navigator cabins, were to be given special attention. Initially, a single aircraft or a range of aircraft types was displayed against a neutral, usually blue, background (Figures 2.13 and 2.14) so that the viewer's attention could be focused uniquely on the aircraft themselves as they might be imagined in flight. Later, as aircraft became more modern and distinctive in their merits, the flying cross sections were placed in a more dynamic context (Figures 2.17 and 2.22). Large airlines such as Air France and Imperial Airways, which operated worldwide using both land- and sea-launched aircraft, often used the poster with cutaway aeroplane sections to show the range as well as the detail of the craft that they operated. So today these posters offer a succinct guide to what might have been seen in the skies of the period and the variety of machines in regular use. In two posters of the late 1930s, these airlines adopt a similar formula

Figure 2.13 Imperial Airways (four aircraft cross sections), late 1930s

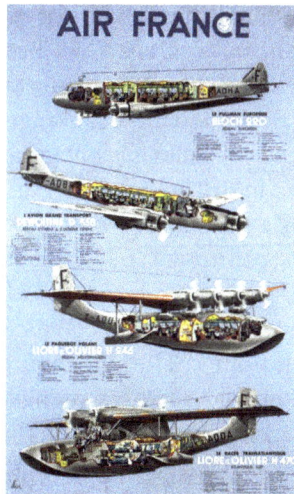

Figure 2.14 Air France (four aircraft cross sections), N. Gérale, 1938

to display aircraft types currently operational, in both cases contrasting land-with seaplanes.

Imperial Airways' consistently asserted commitment to safety and comfort on the long imperial routes is underlined by the choice of four-engined aircraft ('Four engines for safety'), as can be seen by the poster (Figure 2.15) showing

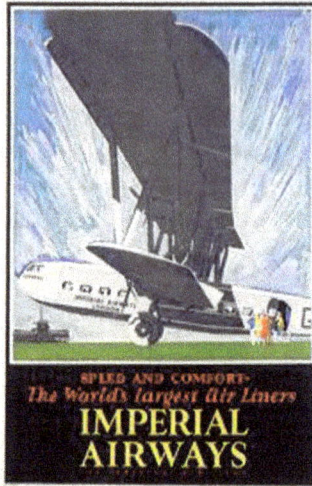

Figure 2.15 Imperial Airways Speed and Comfort (Handley Page HP 42), late 1930s

the giant Handley Page HP 42 (which commenced service in 1931) and the Short Scylla (Figure 2.16), in service from 1934. Both mammoth biplanes are similar in their layout and construction, though the former by far outnumbered the latter, even though the Scylla had more passenger seats, the 26 seats of the HP 42 being set out in a spacious Pullman configuration. Individually, each of these two aircraft is featured in striking Imperial Airways posters of the period (Figures 2.15 and 2.16). The third in the trio of landplanes in Figure 2.13 is the more modern-looking Armstrong Whitworth Atalanta which was used by Imperial Airways from 1933 to transport a dozen and a half people at a time on some of its African routes. The poster is completed by the Short S17 Kent four-engined seaplane that, from 1931 to the outbreak of World War II, was regularly transporting 16 Imperial Airways passengers to the Far East, cruising at 105 mph. However, the most important British flying boat of the 1930s, the Short Canopus 'Empire-class' machine, of which 28 were operational in 1937 (Figure 2.18), does not appear in this poster, though it was given individual attention, as we shall see, in many others of the period, as well as in early BOAC posters of the 1940s.

Like Imperial Airways, Air France was committed to serving the country's colonies in Africa and the Far East, many of which could only be accessed by air using sea or river landing. Before World War II, adequate airstrips outside Europe and North America were rare, either because of difficult terrain or because passenger numbers were insufficient to justify the expense of construction. So reliable long-haul seaplanes such as the Loiré et Olivier H246 and H

Figure 2.16 Imperial Airways (Short Scylla), late 1930s

470, with their four engines and 200 mph cruising speed, were juxtaposed on the same poster (Figure 2.14) with such regular aircraft as the Bloch 220 and Dewoitine D 338, used on both short-haul European and some long-haul imperial routes. Both these planes appear regularly in other Air France posters of the 1930s before they became superseded after 1946 by the new Lockheed Constellation.

The change in approach, after World War II, to aircraft cross section posters is clearly visible in a BOAC poster of the 1940s (Figure 2.17), in which a cut-out section of the stalwart Sandringham Empire flying boat is compared with a distant view of the new Lockheed Constellation. The Canopus-type had been flying the Empire routes since 1932, and 28 of them, as we saw, were operational in 1937 (Figure 2.18). By the late 1940s the now venerable flying boats (of which the Short Sandringham was one of the last) were still flying the flag on British overseas routes, in particular to the Far East; indeed this type, as its close juxtaposition with the Speedbird logo shows, is still the mainstay of the corporation. However, while the new Lockheed Constellation, despite its far superior speed and range, is relegated to the lower part of the poster, it is nevertheless seen as a glimpse of the future in which it will create an even 'smaller world by Speedbird'. Already in this poster, it is the BOAC logo that asserts its pre-eminence over the aircraft portrayed, a trend that will continue throughout the later 1940s and 1950s (see Figures 1.4 and 1.10) as the airline and its destination rather than the manner of conveyance become the focus of attention.

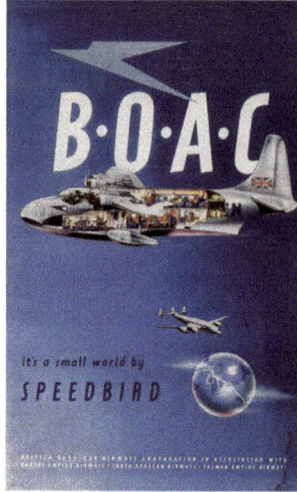

Figure 2.17 BOAC It's a small world by Speedbird (Short Canopus), 1946

Figure 2.18 Imperial Airways 28 Hydravions 'Empire' (Short Canopus), Albert Brenet, 1937

The one notable exception to this shift of focus from the aircraft itself was the spate of posters that appeared between the later 1940s and the 1960s, signalling the arrival of significant new airliners on the post-war European, American and Australian scene. The examples chosen here successively mark the apotheosis of the piston-engined airliner, as in the Lockheed Constellation which entered service in 1946 (Figure 2.19); the arrival of the first and very successful turboprop airliner, the Vickers Viscount, 1953 (Figures 2.20 and 2.21); the dawn of the jet age so beautifully but problematically ushered in by the De Havilland Comet 1 in 1952 (Figure 2.22). The Lockheed Constellation, with its distinctive triple tailplane, was from 1948 to appear on the posters of many international airlines, for example, as in the Qantas poster of c. 1947 (Figure 2.19) that hints at the dominance it was to exert in civil air travel over the following decade. The cut-away profile of the Viscount in an Aer Lingus poster of the mid-1950s (Figure 2.21), in which a plan view of the aircraft appears against the background of the Irish flag, seems to have a double function: familiarizing an increasingly numerous and prosperous Irish clientele with the comforts of air travel and showing that Aer Lingus, the Irish national airline, was now using the latest and most sophisticated aircraft, a far cry from the lone and obsolete De Havilland Dragon that had been the service's mainstay at its initiation in 1937. Finally, the revolutionary Comet 1 (Figure 2.22), powered by four jet engines, was able to halve flight times between destinations and open up the possibility of intercontinental travel in a matter of hours rather than, as previously, days. The speed, smoothness and comfort the aircraft promised are shown in the serene image of it flying above a globe that is, in particular, still tilted to show the British Commonwealth routes that the Comet would continue to serve. From within a decade of this aircraft's introduction, however, jet travel had become banal. Furthermore, after the distinctive variations on jet layout offered in the late 1950s and early 1960s by the Sud Aviation Caravelle, the Boeing 707, the Hawker-Siddley Trident and the Vickers VC10, a standard model of two or four engines in underwing pods became the norm, so that today's airliners, whether they be Airbuses or Boeings, are difficult to differentiate, with only the super-large Boeing 747s and the Airbus A380s able to use their size to assert their difference. This normalization has meant that the aircraft themselves are rarely used as main features in contemporary airline posters. A recent exception was the supersonic Concorde until its withdrawal from service in 2005.

Glamour Destinations

It would be possible to write a whole book about the representation of glamour destinations in airline posters of the 1920–70 period. The focus here, however, is narrowed to key visual tropes used in glamorizing destinations and a case study of the way such tropes evolve over a period of 30 to 40 years. Like the names of capital cities that fashion houses like to exhibit under their trademarks – London – Paris – New York – there are a handful of destinations

Figure 2.19 Qantas Empire Airways: In Australian skies A New Constellation, c. 1947

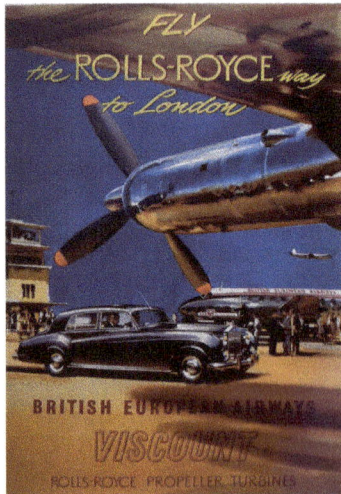

Figure 2.20 BEA Viscount Fly the Rolls-Royce way to London, Frank Wootton, mid-1950s

that no reputable international airline would risk eliminating from their regular scheduled flights. So London, Paris, New York, Rio, Sydney have since the 1930s and 1940s – as jewels in the crown of international travel – had

Figure 2.21 The Aer Lingus Viscount, 1954

Figure 2.22 BOAC Comet Jetliner, 1952

countless posters devoted to advertising their elegance and charm. (Berlin, owing not least to its partition after World War II, never attained this status.) As with other categories of travel poster – the apotheosis of the airline logo, the view from the window, the representation of the exotic – the glamour destination poster tends to be constructed following three or four standard templates that are variously adapted by different airlines. Given the nature of the glamour destination – usually a capital city (national or state), very often set in a striking geographical situation, rich in culture and monuments, a centre of fashion and amusement – the poster designer is often in a quandary as how best to exhibit within one image the delights available. Learning from master poster designers of the 1920s and 1930s such as Cassandre and Jean Carlu, many designers opted for the collage or montage approach which, drawing on cubist and futurist painting and art deco, combined telling visual motifs with which a compelling and aesthetic synthesis could be created.

In the 1950s artists such as Jean Carlu and Jacques Nathan-Garamond created for Air France posters that made an attractive synthesis of the cultural riches of cities such as Paris and Rome. Carlu's Paris poster of 1956 (Figure 2.23) arranges an assortment of Parisian tourist sites around the central image of the Obelisk, subtly incorporating this *ensemble* into a still-life comprising a wineglass, a rose, a theatrical mask and a violin, the totality expressing the cultural wealth and romance of the French capital. In Nathan-Garamond's poster of 1957 (Figure 2.24), a sense of the constant surprise and archaeological richness of Rome is evoked as the viewer's eye is led towards the progressively receding architectural and archaeological elements that constitute the image of the ancient city. For some cities, such as London and New York, the theme of 'the capital by night' was a successful ploy since it enabled the artist to portray in one relatively ill-defined but spectacular image a sense of the lights, movement and excitement of Piccadilly Circus or Times Square. Dick Negus and Philip Sharland made a speciality of this in their mid-1950s posters for BOAC. So, for example, the 1954 BOAC poster promoting Great Britain (Figure 2.25), like the BOAC Rio poster of the same period analysed in Chapter 1 (Figure 1.2), uses a dark, night-time backdrop to some of the signature motifs of the central London scene – the red routemaster bus, the underground railway logo (one of the world's best-known trademarks), even the BOAC Speedbird itself as advertised in neon on the side of a building. For a BOAC North America poster designed by Frank Wootton (Figure 2.26), the bustle of downtown New York is evoked by leading the viewer's eye from the limousines in the foreground cruising the broad streets to the soaring skyscrapers, the blazing lights of traffic and buildings creating an exhilarating vision of life in what was then the largest and most modern North American city.

Among the most successful airline posters promoting glamour destinations are those that combine mimetic or iconic motifs with linguistic elements into a visual syntax that provides a symbolic representation of the country or region in view. Two posters wonderfully illustrate this technique in which a symbolic rather than mimetic approach to the visual icons used enables the latter to take

Figure 2.23 Air France Paris, Jean Carlu, 1956

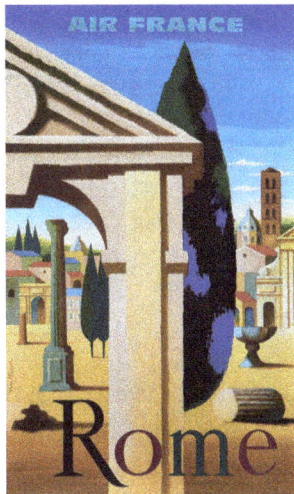

Figure 2.24 Air France Rome, Jacques Nathan-Garamond, 1957

on multiple meanings. In the Pan Am poster of c. 1960 (Figure 2.27), the company logo, with its stylized longitudinal and latitudinal lines within a circle, represents not only the globe across which Pan Am flights travel but also the sun rising in the Far East and an oriental lantern hanging in the dawn or dusk of the Eastern scene. Juxtaposed with the Chinese junk in the foreground and

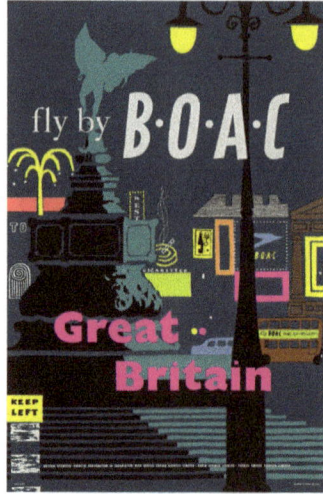

Figure 2.25 Fly by BOAC Great Britain, Dick Negus and Philip Sharland, 1954

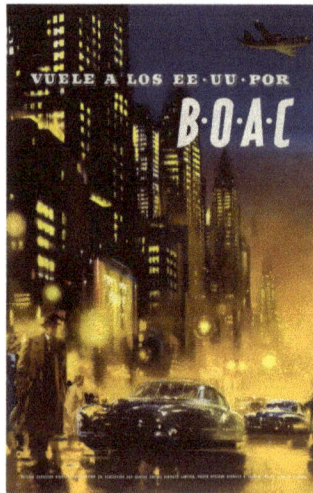

Figure 2.26 Vuele a los EE-UU por BOAC/Fly to USA by BOAC, Frank Wootton, 1950

the high and distant profile of a Boeing 707 jet in the background, the image communicates a highly poetic message about traditional and modern travel in the Far East. A similarly poetic effect is created by a BOAC poster of the same period, also promoting travel to the Far East (Figure 2.28). Here visual

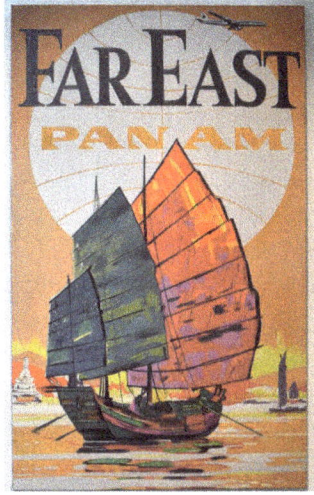

Figure 2.27 Pan Am Far East, c. 1960

Figure 2.28 Fly by BOAC Far East, c. 1960

(iconic) and linguistic (symbolic) elements are juxtaposed in a manner recalling Chinese or Japanese art in which text and image are seamlessly combined. The use in the BOAC poster of Eastern ideogrammatic as well as Western linguistic forms of expression enriches the idea of the meeting of cultures. Once again the use of the oriental lantern motif is most effective: here, it represents both the globe that often accompanies the BOAC acronym in that company's posters (compare Figures 1.4 and 1.10) and a pink moon that casts an eerie light over the exotic landscape that is given substance both by the pagoda and pines and the clumps of Chinese or Japanese ideograms that provide depth and relief to the scene. Few airline travel posters are more seductive than these, still appealing powerfully to the viewer, 60 years after their conception.

The gradual movement from a more conventionally mimetic or descriptive approach to a more radical or artistic synthesis of elements in airline posters evoking glamour destinations is evident in the way the former Brazilian capital of Rio de Janeiro has, as an icon of South America, been presented over four decades (1930s to 1960s). In a poster of the late 1930s designed by Paul George Lawler (Figure 2.29), a conventional formula is employed: the Boeing clipper aircraft is seen flying into Rio over the top of the Christ monument that dominates the (then) Brazilian capital. The prominently placed caption 'Flying down to Rio' reminds the viewer (as if that were necessary) of the glamour and excitement this city has held for Americans, not least since its portrayal in popular song-and-dance movies of the period, the most famous of which was a Fred Astaire and Ginger Rogers film of that title released in 1933. An equally conventional format is used, but to more spectacular effect, by BOAC in a poster of the late 1950s (Figure 2.30) in which the gorgeous greens of the vegetation and the vivid blue of water and sky create a feeling of tropical warmth and intensity of light that is lacking in the rather grey Pan American poster. Both these posters are eclipsed, however, by the BOAC poster (Figure 1.2) discussed in Chapter 1 and by two other more recent posters evoking the Brazilian city. The Varig (Viação Aérea Rio-Grandense, founded in 1927) airline poster of 1950s (Figure 2.31) successfully adopts the Carlu or Cassandre-type of poster design in which a number of spectacular visual motifs are brought together to form an alluring synthesis of the destination's attractions. Against a vivid purple-magenta background, the artist has brought together the tropical delights of Rio (brightly coloured orchids and parrots) with the geographical location (the bay, the Sugarloaf Mountain), a famous monument (the giant Christ figure) and leisure activities (sailing, enjoying the beach) to create a jewel-like synthesis. A similarly vivid approach, this time to the Caribbean, is evident in an Air France poster by Jacques Nathan-Garamond of the same period (Figure 2.32).

Two artists, however, both commissioned by Air France, using Rio as glamour destination, bring the airline poster to a level of aesthetic perfection that has not since been surpassed. The first is by the 1960s Hungarian-born op-artist Victor Vasarely (1906–1997) who in 1946 produced one of the most memorable airline poster images of all time (Figure 2.34), portraying a Lockheed Constellation aircraft making its final approach to the city of Rio

Figure 2.29 Flying down to Rio Pan American Airways, Paul George Lawler, 1930s

Figure 2.30 Fly to South America by BOAC, 1959

de Janeiro across the South Atlantic Ocean. A full moon shining low in the sky casts myriad golden reflections on the sea as the silhouette of the aircraft descends towards the distant shore, the ripples of light unfolding towards the viewer like the pleasures the destination promises. In a similar *tour de force*, in his *Amérique du sud* poster of 1967, the French painter Georges Mathieu

Figure 2.31 Rio VARIG, c. 1955

Figure 2.32 Air France The Caribbean, Jacques Nathan-Garamond, 1960s

(born 1921), commissioned by Air France to produce a series of visual icons representing glamour destinations (such as London, Japan, New York), uses his distinctive calligraphic style and his pyrotechnical skill as a colourist to create an explosive image of the continent (Figure 2.33). Using a palette of warm, dark colours – purple, indigo, black – contrasted with streaks of silver,

Figure 2.33 Air France Amérique du sud, Georges Mathieu, 1967

Mathieu expresses, in a few masterly brushstrokes that fizzle like fireworks, the vitality and exoticism of South America. In posters such as these, Vasarely and Mathieu succeed in creating images that transcend even as they fulfil their immediate function as advertising.

Woman as destination

The sex appeal of a destination only became explicitly spelt out in airline travel posters after World War II. Of course, there had been the occasional hint in pre-war travel posters, especially American ones, that some places were synonymous with exotic sex, Hawaii in particular being marketed from the 1930s onwards almost exclusively in this way. Paul George Lawler's classic Pan American Airlines poster of the 1930s (Figure 2.35) – one of the most popular and sought-after travel posters of all time – set the trend: a massive, phallic Boeing 314 flying boat comes into land in a blue lagoon, surrounded by exotic vegetation and flowers, awaited by a young Hawaiian girl, reclining on the shore in an apparently topless dress, crowned with frangipani. For the major European airlines before 1940, however, foreign travel meant empire business not holiday dalliance and the evocation of destinations in Air France or Imperial Airways' posters reflected this ethos. All was to change after the war, however, when tourism on a mass scale and the use of the aeroplane

Figure 2.34 Air France Amérique du sud, Victor Vasarely, 1946

Figure 2.35 Fly to South Sea Isles via Pan American, Paul George Lawler, 1930s

as a means of holiday travel became increasingly widespread in the Western world. By the late 1950s, the desired holiday prerequisites of sun and sea were more or less blatantly becoming supplemented by the piquant addition of sex, so that even airlines as respectable as BEA and BOAC were using images of females – either indigenous or the European tourist herself – as an enticement to travel.

Initially, the appeal of the erotic female Other in relation to airline travel was rather covertly launched. A BEA poster of 1950 by Percy Drake Brookshaw (Figure 2.36) clothes the sex appeal aspect of various indigenous European female types in a vaguely anthropological or folkloric guise, with traditional costumes and dances (Dutch, Spanish or Italian) making more generally palatable the idea of woman as travel destination. By the later 1950s, however, both BEA and BOAC were presenting unambiguously alluring female figures as the central icons in posters advertising holiday destinations, whether they were Spain (Figure 2.37) or the Caribbean (Figure 2.38). In the BEA poster, the flamenco dancer is smiling invitingly to the viewer, seemingly indicating with a clap of her castanets that she is herself synonymous with the country, Spain, towards the name of which her left hand seems to be gesturing. In the BOAC Caribbean poster, the Carib dancer is lifting her red skirts and white frilled petticoats provocatively to the viewer, the warm colours of the poster perhaps indicating the warmth of the welcome he will receive, the blue of the BOAC acronym being matched by the cummerbund and headscarf that complete the woman's picturesque

Figure 2.36 Fly BEA to the Continent, Percy Drake Brookshaw, 1950

Figure 2.37 Spain fly BEA, 1950s

attire. In both these posters, sex appeal may be seen still to be using local colour as an alibi. A similar strategy is employed in a Swissair poster of 1963 promoting travel to Japan (Figure 2.39) that shows a geisha girl dressed in a scarlet kimono welcoming the visitor with a gesture of her fan. The BOAC poster of the same period advertising travel to South America (Figure 1.2),

Figure 2.38 Nassau Jamaica Fly BOAC, Hayes, 1950s

Figure 2.39 Swissair Japan, 1963

discussed in Chapter 1, though presenting the woman in the alluring setting of Rio at night, does not hide behind the local colour alibi, however, since the carnival itself is a manifestation of sexual exuberance.

When the white holiday-maker herself or, perhaps in the case of Australia, the white Australian female becomes the focus of the poster, the sexual message is without ambiguity. So the beach scene in which a blond, white middle-class 'Rix girl' (a type named after the artist Aubrey Rix who from 1947 to 1951 regularly portrayed women of this type on the covers of *Woman's Own*), in her fetching black and gold bikini, white straw hat and sunglasses, is being pursued by a tall, white, sun-tanned male (Figure 2.40), proposes what would have been for the previous generation a shockingly new way of enticing a young and relatively liberated post-war clientele to enjoy the benefits of air travel to destinations such as the Caribbean islands. A similar though less sophisticated message is communicated by a Qantas/BOAC poster of the same period (Figure 2.41) in which a stereotypical blond in a red swimsuit smiles to a male viewer whose presence may be inferred in the phallic surfboard she is clutching.

After the 1960s, however, such coyness is no longer possible and airline posters, in competition with an increasingly flagrant and all-pervasive dissemination of sexual imagery in the Western world, if they bother at all to stimulate the sexual fantasies of a public by now massively exhorted to indulge their desires, do so as crassly as any other medium. So the British Eagle charter airways poster exhorting its viewers to 'Fly British Eagle to Continental Sun', judging by the young women who flank the phallic tail of the aircraft in the centre of the poster image, may be read as an unambiguous invitation to Continental Sex (Figure 2.42). In comparison, the BOAC Rio poster of the late 1950s celebrated in Chapter 1 (Figure 1.2) seems decidedly discreet, even more so when set alongside a Pan Am poster promoting Rio (Figure 2.43) that caused controversy in the 1970s. As we saw in Chapter 1, Australian Airlines in 1990 launched a series of posters designed to lure the young and upwardly mobile of both genders to the Gold Coast by staging provocative sexual scenarios (Figure 1.1). In the same year, a Western Airline poster presents New York as a line-up of dancing girls, one of whom seems about to be penetrated by the spire of the Empire State Building that forms part of a frieze of skyscrapers along the bottom of the poster, while the vacant eyes of the statue of Liberty stare down impassively from the top of the image (Figure 2.44).

To summarize, sex, as any advertising agent from the early 1950s onwards could have told you, sells anything, and travel is just one of the many consumer objects or services that are so marketed. There is, however, an especially deep link between travel and libido, the possibility of a change of environment bringing with it the chance of new social and sexual opportunities. In an age of mass sex tourism, this aspect of travel becomes a less alluring basis for poster imagery unless, as in the Pan Am Rio poster of the 1970s and that of the Western Airlines New York poster of c. 1990, it parodies as much as

Figure 2.40 Vuele al Mar Caribe por BOAC, Aubrey Rix, 1949–50

Figure 2.41 Australia Fly there by BOAC & Qantas, Hayes, 1953

it promotes its object. Irony, therefore, as in so much of post-modern culture, has become an inescapable part of advertising, providing an alibi for what otherwise might have been viewed as vulgarity or bad taste. In such an age, calculating the right measure of fantasy to supplement the information that a

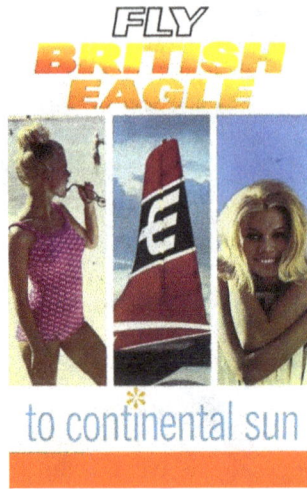

Figure 2.42 Fly British Eagle to Continental Sun, 1960s

Figure 2.43 Pan Am Rio Experience makes the difference, 1970s

Figure 2.44 Western Airlines New York, 1990

poster is generally supposed to supply is a tricky business. With so much media competition, the airline poster rarely finds the time or space to create the kind of subtly alluring image that in the past it was able to produce, one for which, even in the hyper-sophisticated twenty-first century, we nevertheless retain a certain nostalgia.

Chapter 3

LOOKING OUT AND LOOKING UP: FRAMING DEVICES AND INDEXICAL SIGNS

A poster is not structured like a picture: having more in common with a postage stamp, it is an indexical as much as an iconic sign in that it points to a specific official or commercial message rather than merely presenting a mimetic image. This indexical dimension is manifested in the text that accompanies it, even if it is as minimal as a logo or the name of an airline. This fact is often overlooked by viewers who have become so used to the poster format that they are no longer conscious of the double nature of its structure as a sign. So, the poster by its very nature combines an alluring visual image or *icon*, with a textual clue – what Roland Barthes (1964) described as *ancrage* or anchorage for the image's meaning. The art of the poster lies in the combination of the iconic (visual) and indexical (textual) message, a synthesis that is enhanced if the symbolic elements that constitute the indexical message (the letters or language used) are seamlessly combined with the iconic or pictorial element. In those rare successful poster campaigns that rely solely on a fine photographic image (as in the Pan Am series of the 1960s), the airline logo and/or name is sufficient in itself to *anchor* the image in a context that enables the meaning of the image to be grasped. So, in Figure 3.1, the assumed message is: the airline Pan Am flies regularly to such exotic destinations as Bali.

In the light of this, most airline posters combine a pictorial image (usually that of the proposed destination viewed as a landscape, a monument, an indigenous type or a collage or montage of several stereotypical images) and a fragment of text which usually includes the name of the airline, its logo and any slogan associated with it ('It's a smaller world by Speedbird: BOAC'; 'Dans tous les ciels: Air France'). Additionally, in the early days of commercial flying and scheduled flights (from the 1920s to the 1940s) it was usual to include the image of an aircraft (or even two if the airline operated flying boats as well as regular planes). This aircraft image would be sited in the sky of the advertised destination or on approach to it or at the point of take-off; alternatively, it would itself provide the context from which the destination or the

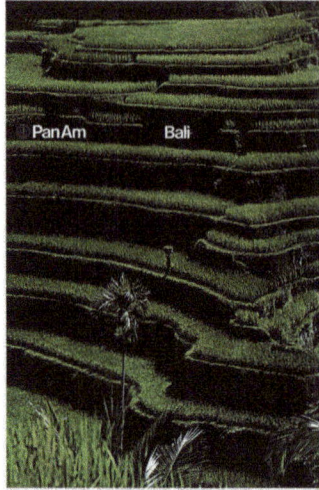

Figure 3.1 Pan Am Bali, Ivan Chermayeff, Thomas Geismar, 1972

approach to it could be viewed. This chapter will focus in particular on the use in early airline posters of these two indexical strategies in order to show both the tension between information and desire inherent in the poster image and the way the inclusion of the aircraft as viewed, or as vantage point for viewing, became an important part of the poster's persuasive strategy.

The aircraft image can be integrated in varying degrees of complexity into the poster design, ranging from its simple appearance in the distant sky to its depiction flying low over or at the point of landing (at the destined airport or seaplane docking point). It can also be integrated into a visual allegory in which it may serve to communicate a specific message relating to a destination or speak more generally about the airline itself (as in the Air France poster analysed in Figure 1.3). The advantage of the first option is that the larger part of the poster can be devoted to lavishly depicting an exotic destination that the poster viewer enters into with minimal distraction, imagining they are already being magically transported there by the aircraft glimpsed in the distant sky. This ploy is effectively exploited by many airlines including Air India (Figure 3.2), Qantas/BOAC (Figure 3.3) and Air France (Figure 3.4).

If the foreign aircraft is depicted being spotted by a person indigenous to the destination, a quite different and indeed ambivalent, interpretative dynamic is activated. As this situation forms part of the wider question of the reception by natives of Western colonial or commercial intrusion into their lands and skies, it will be dealt with more fully in Chapter 4. However, as the 'indigenous' viewer is sometimes a colonial or former colonial, the message

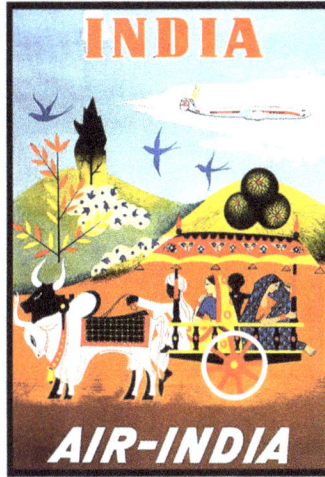

Figure 3.2 Air-India, India, 1950s

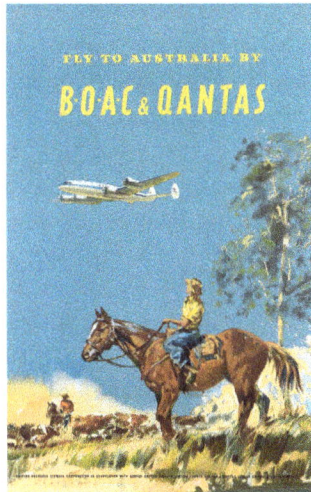

Figure 3.3 Fly to Australia by BOAC & Qantas, Frank Wootton, 1950

communicated by his (it is usually his, not her) upward gaze at the approaching BOAC, Air France or Qantas aircraft may be interpreted in a less specifically colonialist or imperialist way. So one is led to wonder whether the handsome sunburned white Australian depicted in Harold Foster's BOAC/Qantas poster of the later 1940s (Figure 3.5) lifts his muscular arm to adjust his akubra as a

Figure 3.4 Air France Far East, Vincent Guerra, 1949

visor to the sun or in a gesture of salute to the incoming aircraft. The intention is probably to suggest both. Similarly, the figure of a turbaned Indian in another BOAC poster of the same period and series (Figure 3.6) is presumably intended (India having achieved its independence in 1947) to express the idea of mutual equality and respect between independent member states of the British Commonwealth of Nations.

The closer the aircraft or flying boat depicted in the poster comes to its destination, the more alluring the scene tends to become as it supplies the potential traveller with the exotic detail of the arrival that will have a powerful impact on their imagination. So, the Imperial Airways Handley Page 42 that in its landing approach is flying over an Indian riverside city (Figure 3.7) provides a commanding view of the destination in which the thriving urban and riverine activity of the natives is glimpsed in radiant sunshine. This kind of image may be interpreted as inferring a colonialist message as the viewer of the scene (whether imagined to be aboard the aircraft or to be looking at the poster from the outside) projects a potentially imperialist gaze over the territory and people to which Imperial Airways are (or may be) delivering them. A similar approach is adopted in a classic Paul George Lawler-designed poster for Pan American clipper arriving in Hong Kong (Figure 3.8) in which the exotic destination of Cathay is set out in colourful detail. Even more fascinating (and proportionately more ideologically problematic) are those scenes of arrival of Imperial Airways flying boats (Figures 3.9 and 3.10) of the 1930s and 1940s that, having touched down at their maritime or estuarine point

Figure 3.5 BOAC/QEA Speedbird routes across the world, Harold Foster, 1946

Figure 3.6 BOAC Speedbird routes over the Atlantic and across the world, Harold Foster, 1946

Figure 3.7 India by Imperial Airways, W. H. A. Constable, c. 1935

of landing, are surrounded by native craft and people eager to transport to the mainland the Western passengers and goods delivered by the airline. The presence of both regular aircraft and flying boats (Figure 3.10) advertises the options open to the colonial or tourist traveller while also discreetly making the point that British imperial power controls both sky and sea.

Figure 3.8 Transpacific Flight Pan American Airways, Paul George Lawler, 1930s

Figure 3.9 Imperial Airways 28 Hydravions type 'Empire', Albert Brenet, 1937

An additional glamour can be bestowed on the exotic destination when it is viewed at night, as in the KNILM poster of 1932 (a possible visual intertext to the paddy-field view offered by the Pan Am Bali poster in Figure 3.1) in which the dark shape of the KNILM aircraft as it flies over the rice fields is silhouetted against the tropical night sky (Figure 3.11).

Figure 3.10 Fly to the Far East BOAC, Rowland Hilder, c. 1948

Figure 3.11 KNILM Royal Netherlands Indian Airways, 1932

When the aircraft (or in the case of Imperial Airways/BOAC, the famous Speedbird logo) is incorporated into an allegorical framework, it becomes as much an expression of the general ethos of the airline company in question as a message about specific destinations. In such posters (Figures 1.4, 1.10 and 1.11), the aircraft or airline logo is juxtaposed with the world (represented as either a map or a globe) rather than a specific destination within it, the message being that the airline in question covers the earth in its entirety, offering routes to all the major international destinations. As we saw in Chapter 1, the aim of this approach was to tempt the poster viewer into the myth of the major airlines' domination of world travel and to be persuaded that modern advances in aeronautical technology indeed enable the individual to travel rapidly and safely anywhere on earth. No poster illustrates this point better than a Pan Am Far East poster of c. 1960 (Figure 2.27) in which the Pan Am logo (a globe with stylized latitudinal and longitudinal lines) rises in place of the eastern sun over a junk sailing in the China Sea.

The second major category of airline poster image incorporating the aircraft is that of the 'armchair traveller' type. No doubt adapted from early twentieth-century railway travel posters, it aims to emphasize both the comfort of modern air travel and the unique point of vantage the porthole offers to a passenger on an airborne craft. Imperial Airways, as part of its strategy during the 1920s and 1930s of highlighting the luxurious style of travel their flying boats and regular aircraft provided, were the first to use this motif repeatedly. So an Imperial Airways Comfort Routes poster of the 1920s (Figure 3.12) imagines the single passenger to be ensconced among the clouds in a winged armchair. Smoking his cigarette, the passenger resembles the member of any London gentleman's club, the service offered by the airline, like that of the club, being so deferential and discreet that there is no need to represent it. A slightly later Imperial Airways poster, 'By Air in Comfort to Europe, Africa, Asia' (Figure 3.13), offers a similar message. Here the focus on the comfort of the passenger is such that the presence of the air steward is partly obliterated, the viewer's attention being caught in particular by the way the textual message of the poster, with its sans serif art deco typography, harmonizes with the simplified forms of the visual image. In Imperial Airways posters from the later 1920s, the excellence of the cabin service is shown to be extended to the elegant clientele of both sexes who were increasingly to travel by air. For example, in Figures 3.14 and 3.15, we see smartly dressed stewards moving down the aisle to serve drinks and refreshments to comfortably seated passengers. Air hostesses only played key role as cabin crew in British airlines after World War II; their contribution to the glamour and comfort of travel is explored in Chapter 5.

From the start, however, the view out of the cabin was as important, if not more important, than the view within and was represented by many posters as a key attraction of airline travel. In an early Lufthansa poster (Figure 3.16), passengers observe from the security and comfort of their airline seats the wintry landscape beneath, the passage of second aircraft passing below over the snow emphasizing the alluring aspect of flight to new air travellers. The

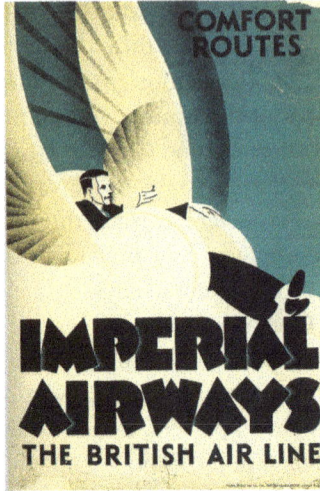

Figure 3.12 Imperial Airways Comfort Routes, 1930

Figure 3.13 By air in comfort to Europe Africa Asia by Imperial Airways, Steph Cavallero, 1937

large, rectangular windows of early aircraft offer themselves as landscape-framing devices similar to those of railway carriage windows, with the additional advantage of height as well as speed to offer new perspectives on the world outside. More often in the 1930s and 1940s, however, it was a single

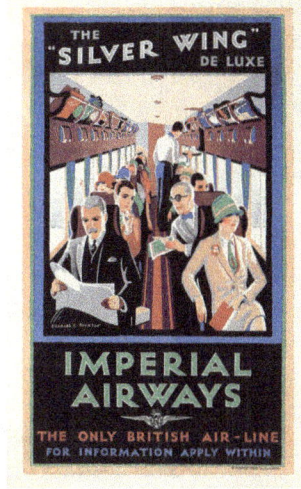

Figure 3.14 Imperial Airways The Silver Wing deluxe, Charles C. Dixon, 1920s

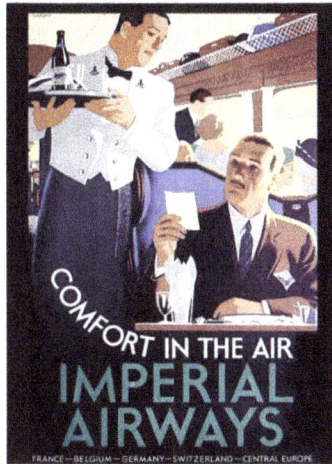

Figure 3.15 Imperial Airways Comfort in the air, 1920s

male passenger who was portrayed viewing the landscape below as the travelling colonial administrator or company executive might be imagined to be already rehearsing the managerial control they would shortly be exerting over the landscape below. In a Pan American Airways poster of the 1930s designed by Kerne Erickson (Figure 3.17), the white-suited American in his boater hat

Figure 3.16 Lufthansa Auch im Winter, Hans Vogel, 1932

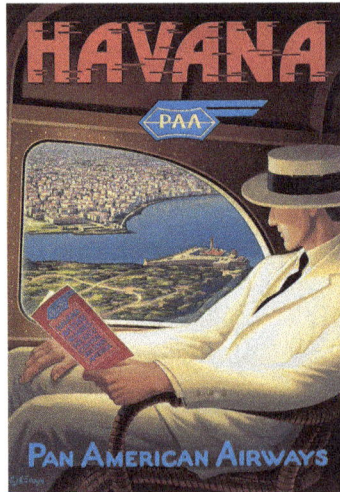

Figure 3.17 Pan American Airways Havana, Kerne Erickson, 1930s

is checking his guidebook as he looks out of the aircraft window as it flies over the port of Havana, his destination.

An Air Afrique poster of 1936 (Figure 3.18), a classic in this genre designed by A. Roquin, is telling not only in itself but also in the way it constitutes an element in a wider, colonial narrative that this airline's promotional posters

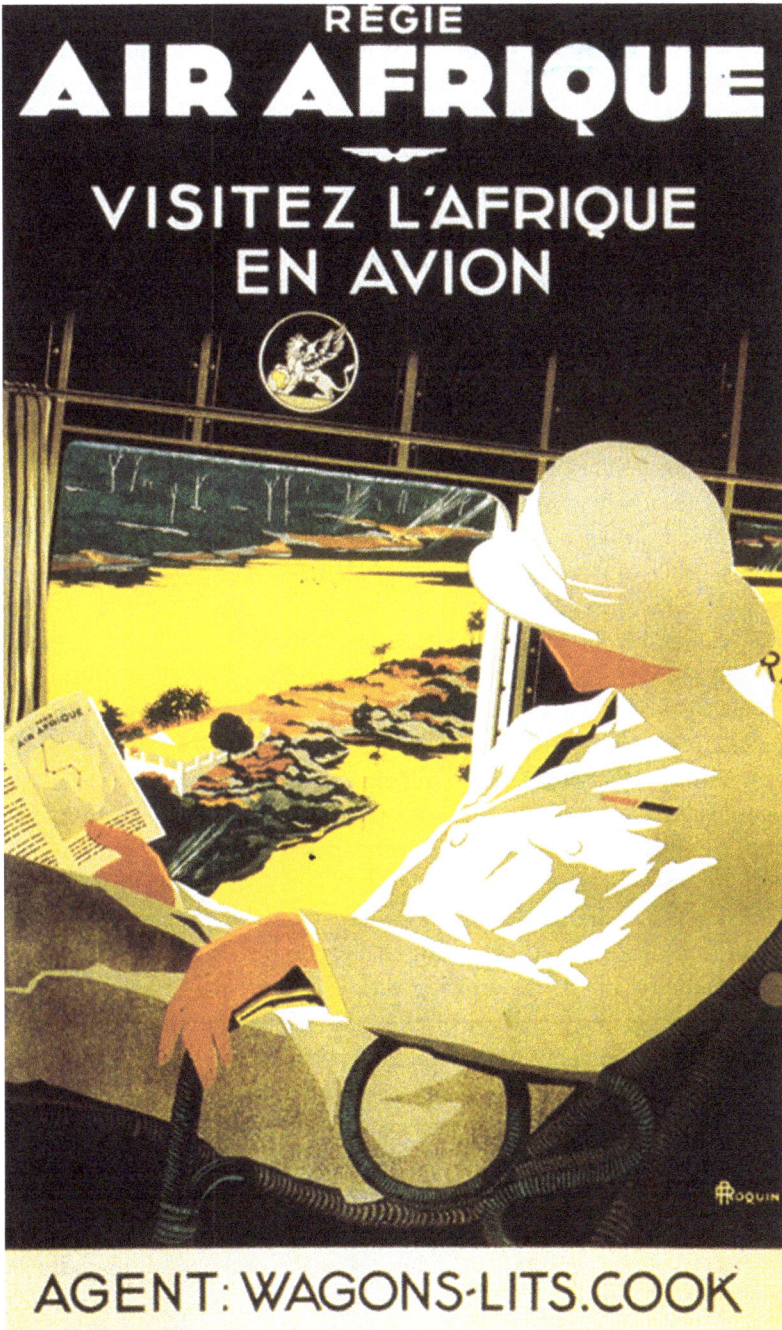

Figure 3.18 Air Afrique Visitez l'Afrique en avion, A. Roquin, 1936

were elaborating at the height of the French colonial development in Africa in the mid-1930s (compare Figure 3.19, also designed by Roquin). In the first poster (Figure 3.18) we see the young French colonial administrator, kitted out in requisite tropical uniform with pith helmet, stretching out in his rattan chair, following from a map unfolded on his knee the Air Afrique itinerary that has delivered him from Algeria to the Congo, with the African river scene viewed from the aircraft porthole. The way the young officer is portrayed to the viewer from behind invites the latter to share his dominating perspective and to enter into the adventure and excitement both of air travel and the imperial project of which, in the 1930s, it was still very much implicated. The second poster, by the same artist (Figure 3.19), may be imagined to portray the same young *colon*, by now established in his administrative functions; in shirt-sleeve order in the heat and pith-helmeted, he now awaits news from home and the military or administrative instructions from his headquarters in Paris, both of which will be delivered by Air Afrique safely and punctually. Comparable colonial narratives were elaborated in French colonial postage stamps of the same period, delivering similarly ambivalent and seductive messages (see Scott, 1995, 2002).

The view from the aircraft window or porthole was as early as the mid-1930s but more commonly in the 1940s to be shared by the whole family as it became possible, at least for the rich, to travel as a family group to certain major destinations. In an Imperial Airways poster of the 1930s (Figure 3.20), there seem to be at least three generations of possibly the same family enjoying the facilities of the aircraft's promenade deck, as the silver-haired lady and her distinguished-looking husband look on as younger passengers, including a school-age girl, stretch their legs and enjoy the view from the aircraft window. In American airline ads of the late 1940s and early 1950s, the nuclear family (father, mother, son and daughter) were shown continuing their normal domestic life while enjoying the view from the airliner window. In a United Airlines magazine ad of the early 1950s the father, in stereotypical masculine connivance, is pointing out to the son a locomotive travelling below that the aircraft is overtaking. In a Trans Australian Airline poster of c. 1958, the advantage of the recently introduced Vickers Viscount's large oval windows is shown as a smartly dressed couple enjoy the view as the aircraft passes over Sydney Harbour Bridge as an ocean-going liner passes beneath it (Figure 3.21).

As aircraft got faster and flew higher, the privileged sight through the porthole window became less a glimpse of passing landscape or preview of destination than a view of the increasingly powerful engines propelling the aircraft. So in a TWA poster of the 1950s (Figure 3.22) the poster viewer and the aircraft passenger are treated to a glimpse of whirling propellers as the aircraft

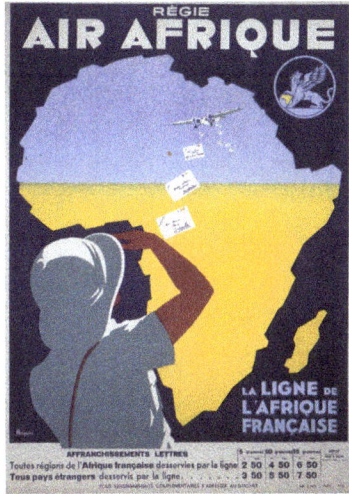

Figure 3.19 Air Afrique La Ligne de l'Afrique française, A. Roquin, 1935

Figure 3.20 Luxury in the new Empire Flying-Boats Imperial Airways, 1930s

flies above the Grand Canyon, while in a classic 1960s Swissair poster by Manfred Bingler (Figure 3.23), it is the jet engines of the recently introduced Convair 990A airliner that become the focus of admiring attention through the porthole.

Figure 3.21 TAA proudly presents the Vickers Viscount, c. 1958

Figure 3.22 TWA Flies Direct Grand Canyon, 1950s

The thrill of greater speed and ease of transport that air travel offered was a factor that motivated another distinctive trope of airline travel promotion, that of the comparison of the aircraft with earlier paradigms of transport such as the sailing ship, the liner, the stagecoach or the car. In 1933, Lufthansa produced a picture showing Junkers Ju-52 airliner flying above a stagecoach

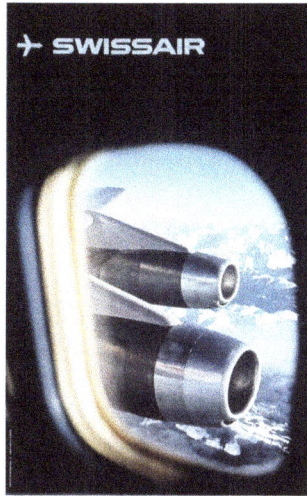

Figure 3.23 Swissair (Convair 990A), Manfred Bingler, 1962

(Figure 3.24) while the Royal Dutch Airline, KLM (founded in 1922), was among the first to exploit the image of a mythical transport archetype in the promotion of modern airline travel (Figures 3.25–3.29) by juxtaposing a sixteenth- or seventeenth-century Dutch galleon with a modern KLM airliner. Drawing on the Flying Dutchman myth, this image reminded the potential air traveller of the long and successful history of the Dutch as a maritime trading nation and its extensive trading contacts, stretching from the East Indies (today's Indonesia) to Surinam in South America. With the onset of air travel in the twentieth century, the Netherlands, like Britain, was eager to maintain its major role in world trade and transport by developing both the technology and the airline networks necessary to exert its traditional dominance and prestige in these domains.

In this context, Croydon Airport, opened in 1920, the antecedent to London Heathrow Airport that was developed after World War II on the basis of a former RAF station, was to become as potentially important a port of egress for British travellers as Liverpool or Southampton (Figure 3.30). Hudson and Pettifer report that by 1938 Croydon Airport was handling 2,000 passengers per day in 40 to 50 take-offs and landings (1979: 106). Croydon was in the 1930s the point of departure of many London to Paris flights, used not only by businessmen but also by the well-heeled of either sex who wished to avail of the swift passage to Paris – as the fashionable, aristocratic Lucy Tantamount character in Aldous Huxley's *Eyeless in Gaza* (1936) confirms. The accessibility of Paris from London and the enhancement of its popularity as

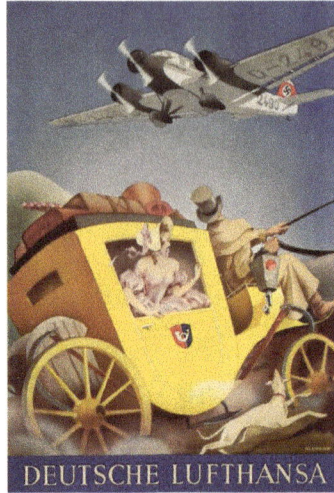

Figure 3.24 Deutsche Lufthansa (Ju 52), Gayle Ullmann, 1933

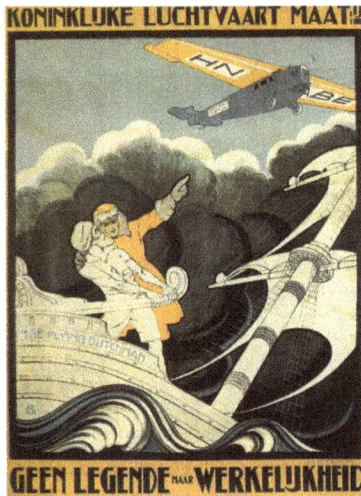

Figure 3.25 KLM Royal Dutch Airlines Geen Legende maar werkelijkheid, M. Güthschmidt, 1920

a glamour destination were enhanced in the 1950s with the introduction of a new generation of turboprop airliners such as the Vickers Viscount. The exceptional smoothness of these new aircraft led them to be compared with the best cars of the age, as we saw in Chapter 2 in a memorable poster of the

Figure 3.26 KLM The Flying Dutchman: Fiction becomes Fact, 1926

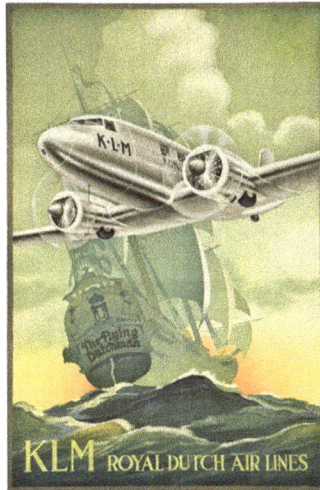

Figure 3.27 KLM Royal Dutch Airlines, Arjen Galema, 1930s

mid-1950s in which the prestige of the world-famous British company Rolls-Royce as a manufacturer both of luxury cars and first-class aero engines was promoted: in a London airport setting, the poster juxtaposes a Viscount, the first operational Rolls-powered turboprop airliner, with a Rolls-Royce Silver Cloud saloon car (Figure 2.20).

Figure 3.28 KLM Lucht Express Holland-Engeland, Huibert G. Brian, 1920s

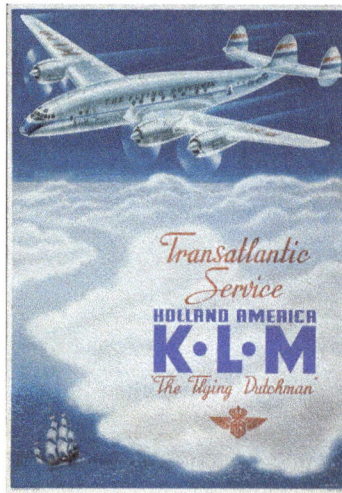

Figure 3.29 KLM Transatlantic Service Holland-America, Paul Erkelens, 1946–47

A similar theme is explored in two posters of the late 1930s: in a 1938 British poster an Armstrong-Whitworth Ensign airliner roars into take-off above a couple who have parked their elegant sports tourer (possibly a Lagonda) to watch the airliner get airborne (Figure 3.31) while 'Les Voyageurs modernes' (Figure 3.32) juxtaposes a sleek Renault sports car of the later 1930s with

Figure 3.30 Imperial Airways (Croydon Airport), Harold McReady, 1920s

Figure 3.31 Armstrong-Whitworth Ensign and motorcar, 1938

a contemporary Caudron-Renault light aircraft. A similarly contemporary juxtaposition of aircraft with alternative means of modern transport was made in an Air Algérie poster of the 1940s showing a Douglas DC4 airliner flying over the Mediterranean above a liner (Figure 3.33), while in a poster of around 1930 a Salvatore Castelli air and terrestrial transport poster shows an

Figure 3.32 Les Voyageurs modernes (Renault motorcar and Caudron-Renault aircraft), late 1930s

Figure 3.33 Paris-Lyon-Marseille pour Alger-Oran Cie générale de transports aériens – Air Algérie, Michel Lezla, 1953

aircraft flying above an express train and a long-distance lorry (Figure 3.34). Overall, the aim of these posters was to promote the idea of both tradition and

Figure 3.34 Salvatore Castelli Transporti aerei e terrestri, Plinio Codognato, c. 1933

continuity in national excellence in the transport field and the international prestige and importance of airline travel in the modern world.

Chapter 4

INDIGENOUS PEOPLES

Airline posters of the interwar period of the twentieth century constitute as rich a source of insight into European colonialist propaganda as any other cultural production. As in postage stamps (see Scott, 1995: 73–85; 2002: 45–53), their primary function – a sign of mail and place of posting for stamps; a sign of destination and means of travel for airline posters – is supplemented more or less subtly by a range of colonialist themes including sexual voyeurism, exoticism, racial fascination and developmental zeal, designed to appeal to the Western (and in particular the Western male) viewer. These themes are mostly presented under the cover of a scientific alibi provided by ethnography, a discipline that burgeoned in Europe in the nineteenth and early twentieth centuries, precisely as the continent's colonial enterprise was reaching its peak. Ethnographic study sets out to analyse and classify the variety of native types; their customs, myths and rituals; and their natural environment. The privileging of the naked or near-naked native body as a focus of attention activated a process that could become, when the images were decontextualized, as rich a source of imaginative reverie as of objective knowledge. Ethnographic discourse and visual documentation are thus prone to be used as a cover for sexual fantasy as well as for economic domination and racial prejudice. The aim of this chapter will be to explore the way such strategies are exploited in interwar French and British airline posters, using as a point of comparison the elaboration of similar themes in 1920s and 1930s stamps issued by these countries' African colonies.

Although Africa (with the exception of Cape Town) lacks the glamorous cities of other equatorial, tropical or subtropical continents – Rio in South America, Hong Kong in the Far East, Sydney in Australia – it makes up for it by a multitude of destinations offering a range of exotic settings – jungle, river, lakeside village, palm-fringed shore. Such sites quickly became the staple settings of interwar airline poster images produced by Britain and France as they sought to give colour and substance to the strange names – Bamako, Dakar, Togo – that the colonial itineraries of their national airlines served. But the airline poster's main appeal was, as in the postage stamps of the interwar colonial period, primarily built around their presentation of native types – naked or semi-naked, male or female – involved in ritual or traditional activities. A fascination with the muscularity or athleticism of the African male is therefore stimulated by depictions of the indigenous body involved in strenuous exercise – propelling a dug-out canoe with a pole, drawing the string of a heavy bow prior to releasing a piercing arrow, running fleet-footedly along a jungle path – while the graceful robustness of the indigenous female form is shown to great advantage in the water jar carrier, the tribal dancer or even the figure peacefully reclining in a hammock slung between palm trees. The uninhibited exposure of male loins and of female breasts is a much-repeated visual trope in both stamps and posters of this kind.

In the majority of colonial stamps, particularly those issued by France, the accurately engraved image of naked or near-naked human forms is enough, beneath the glaze of seeming ethnological objectivity, to stimulate the curiosity, fantasy, even desire, of the viewer and thus motivate adherence, either active or passive, to the colonial enterprise. The airline poster, on the other hand, like airmail postage stamps, needs in addition to such more or less flagrant eroticism to introduce the functionally determining motif of the aircraft that will either deliver the mail to which the stamp is attached or the passenger – colonial, commercial and, after World War II, touristic – to their destination. The juxtaposition of aeroplane or part of an aircraft with indigenous body or native scene thus becomes the standard pictorial trope of posters of this period promoting European travel in and to Africa.

An early and somewhat naïve example of this trope can be seen in an Imperial Airways poster of the mid-1930s: 'Africa by Imperial Airways' (Figure 4.1a). Here a picturesque scene illustrates daily life in what may be assumed to be a typical African community, in which the indigenous population are depicted as offering a smiling welcome to the viewer and, by extension, the future visitor. The presence of bare-breasted African women will become a standard feature of airline posters of the colonial period, as indeed it does in contemporary stamps, though in the latter the ethnographic alibi is usually stronger. This is scarcely the case, however, in Guyane française stamp of 1947 (Figure 4.1b), designed by Raoul Serres, which presents a finely engraved image of life in French Guiana in South America: a naked indigenous female in the foreground lolls languorously in a hammock against a background of a native village scene.

Other airline posters and colonial airmail stamps of the period tend to present a more complex medley of themes, bringing together in one colourful

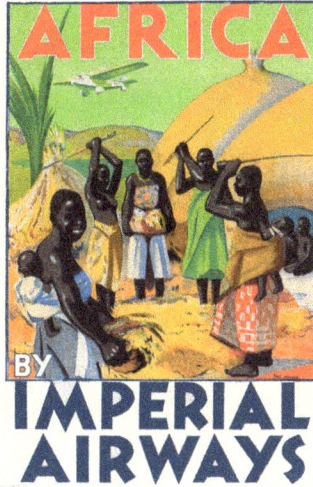

Figure 4.1a Africa by Imperial Airways, 1930s

Figure 4.1b Guyane française 1947, design/engraving Raoul Serres

image the idea of travel, the variety of exotic destinations, the attractiveness of the indigenous types likely to be encountered on arrival and, above all, their relative accessibility. So, in a colourful Imperial Airways poster of the late 1930s (Figure 4.2a), the British Canopus-class flying boat has landed on the blue waters of an African lake or seashore where it is greeted by both a modern transfer launch and a traditional dug-out canoe with its black boatman. The scene is viewed by a young native woman whose charming hibiscus-crowned profile is turned away from the palm-fringed craft to the viewer of the poster in what may be construed as an enticing gesture of welcome. In an airmail stamp from French Cameroun of the following decade (Figure 4.2b), the 75th

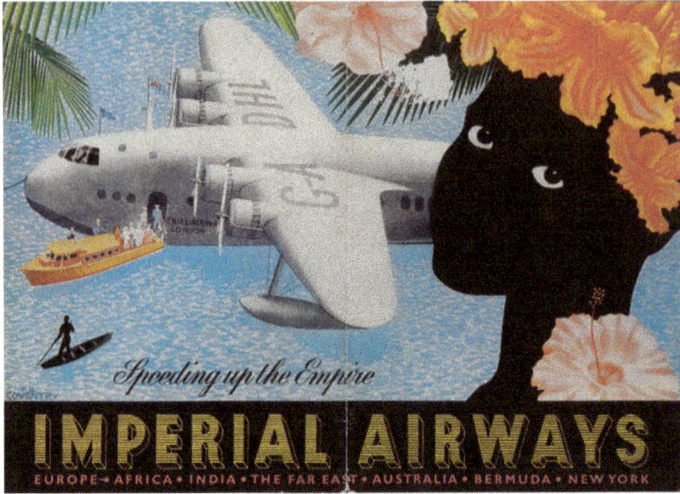

Figure 4.2a Imperial Airways Speeding up the Empire, 1930s

Figure 4.2b Cameroun 1949, 75th anniversary of UPU, design/engraving Raoul Serres

anniversary of the Universal Postal Union is the alibi for a picturesque display of indigenous types ranging from the flower-bedecked Polynesian to the impressively muscular African warrior. In this example, the aircraft (the new Lockheed Constellation) is seen flying high overhead against the background of the globe.

A complex juxtaposition of a comparable sort is provided by a Sabena poster (Figure 4.3a) and another Cameroun stamp (Figure 4.3b), both of the 1940s. In the stamp three powerfully evocative images – aircraft propeller, indigenous warrior and native mask – are juxtaposed, creating a synthesis in which it is suggested that modern aeronautical power can deliver magic in a way similar to that conjured by tribal ritual (symbolized by the mask), the beneficiary of both being marked by the young African warrior. In the Sabena

Figure 4.3a Belgique, Congo belge, Afrique du Sud par Sabena, 1940s

Figure 4.3b Cameroun 1946, design/engraving Institut de gravure/Georges Bétemps

poster, the splendid African head, haloed with a traditional headdress resembling the rays of a black sun, is juxtaposed with a four-engined airliner darkly silhouetted against a cerulean sky.

A similarly suggestive assemblage, this time in the feminine register, is provided by an Imperial Airways poster of this period (Through Africa in days instead of weeks, Figure 4.4a) in which the statuesque perfection of a tall African woman placing a large and heavy jar on her elegantly poised head is set off against the sturdy British load-carrying Speedbird aircraft. Here, the

Figure 4.4a Imperial Airways Through Africa in days instead of weeks, 1930s

Figure 4.4b Senegal 1938, design/engraving Institut de gravure

implied message of strength united with elegance is upstaged by the flagrant eroticism of the image in which even the prow of the aircraft is sexualized through juxtaposition with the African woman's pointed breasts. A similar pose is portrayed by a young Senegalese woman in an Afrique orientale fran-çaise stamp of 1938 (Figure 4.4b).

In what is perhaps the most striking of all the posters in this series is the image presented by the Aeromaritime company in its advertisement for west African coastal routes (Figure 4.5a). In this poster, a magnificently muscled indigenous archer draws the string of a huge bow to release an arrow that will, it is implied, reach its destination with a promptness and accuracy similar to that

Figure 4.5a Aeromaritime Côte occidentale d'Afrique, 1930s

Figure 4.5b Cameroun 1946, design/engraving Albert Decaris

of the Aeromaritime aircraft that flies in the same direction above. The tension of the bowstring as it is powerfully drawn by the archer matches that of the aircraft wings as they sustain the power of the aircraft's motors, the pilot of the craft being imagined to exert the same focus and concentration as the warrior below. A similarly powerful image of the native archer is provided in a Cameroun stamp of 1946 (Figure 4.5b) designed by Albert Decaris in which the arrow is poised to fly out of the stamp's picture frame to strike an unidentified target.

A similar parallel between postage stamp and poster representations of indigenous types can be seen in the Air France Afrique Occidentale française

Figure 4.6a Air France Afrique occidentale, Albert Brenet, 1949

Figure 4.6b Dahomey 1941, design/engraving Albert Decaris

poster of 1949 designed by Albert Brenet (Figure 4.6a) and the Dahomey (Afrique Occidentale française) stamp designed by Albert Decaris earlier in the same decade (Figure 4.6b). In the two images, the postures of the muscular black natives are mirror images of each other, supplemented in the poster by the dead tiger and the young black boy, an addition that suggests the possibility of big-game hunting as an added motivation for travel to French West Africa. In both cases the dug-out canoe is being propelled vigorously out of the picture frame towards the viewer, emphasizing the immediacy and proximity of action: this is particularly apparent in the poster whose image transcends that of the (merely) ethnographic (as in the stamp) to invite active participation on

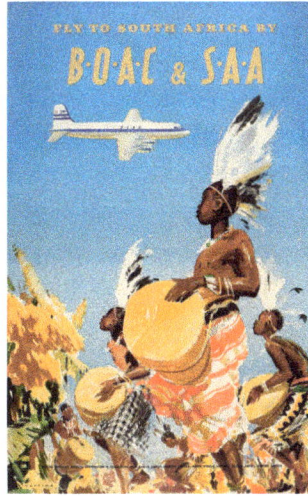

Figure 4.7a Fly to South Africa by BOAC and SAA, c. 1950

the part of the viewer (and potential air traveller). The distant silhouette in the top right-hand corner of the Air France Douglas DC4 aircraft is a discreet reminder of the agent of the viewer's possible entry in real terms into the exotic scene depicted.

In a BOAC & SAA (South African Airlines) poster of c. 1950 (Figure 4.7a), a native band of drummers beat what the viewer construes to be a welcome to the new Handley Page Hermes aircraft that flies through a brilliant sky above the native scene. The vivid colour and upward-looking perspective on both aspects of the image (foreground with native figures, sky with aircraft) seem to bring to the same visual plane the modern and the exotic, expressing the idea that Africa and its native customs are now an integral part of the modern (post-World War II) world. A similar message is communicated by the 1947 Togo airmail stamp in which the native runner delivers the post, attached to a staff he is carrying, to the airport from where it will be collected by the Air France Douglas DC4 seen in the sky above as it lands after its flight from Paris. The theme of native postal runners and modern mail delivery is often portrayed in French colonial stamps of the 1930s and 1940s (see Scott, 2002: 45–53; 2020: 351–59).

A warm welcome to European arrivals in Africa also seems to be extended in an Air Afrique Ligne de Bamako poster of the late 1930s (Figure 4.8a). This shows a Caudron C445 Goéland (which came into service in this period) flying into land above a group of West African natives in full tribal regalia, who

Figure 4.7b Togo 1947, design/engraving Institut de gravure/Pierre Camors

Figure 4.8a Air Afrique Ligne de Bamako, 1930s

are seemingly greeting it with open arms. This sort of relatively unproblematic embrace of modernity in French African colonies is also illustrated by a standard set of airmail stamps issued for all free French colonies from London in 1943 (Figure 4.8b). It was commissioned by General de Gaulle during his wartime exile in Britain. This series was revolutionary not only in its content (the ultra-modern Lockheed Constellation airliner due to enter service after 1946 to French colonies all over the African continent) but also in its radically new design: the celebrated French/British graphic designer Edmund Dulac adopts the new technique of photogravure to striking effect to portray in deep and vivid colour within a modern and yet philatelically coherent design the embrace of freedom and modernity by France's African partners.

Figure 4.8b Madagascar 1943, design/photogravure Edmund Dulac

From the later 1950s and into the early 1960s when British and French colonies in Africa were beginning to gain their independence, the representation of the indigenous population of the countries inevitably had to change. Even the alibi of ethnography was, after World War II, no longer seen as valid, so there was a shift in focus from native types to cultural artefacts, the most privileged of which was the African mask or sculpture. These latter forms had by this time already been fully integrated in the European aesthetic tradition in the light of the work of Cubist artists such as Picasso and Braque at the beginning of the twentieth century. So, an Air France poster of 1960 by Jacques Nathan-Garamond (Figure 4.9a) presents Africa in the form of a wooden sculpture which in its colourful complexity expresses the richness of indigenous culture. A similar strategy was adopted by former French colonies in their post-independence stamps, such as the set issued in 1960 by the République de Haute-Volta which, in the example shown, depicts a Phacochœrus mask (Figure 4.9b). Here the value and the interest of the object displayed are taken as self-evident, as much an enrichment to Western culture as it is of its sacred or ritual significance in its native context.

It is striking that it was particularly airline posters promoting African travel that in the interwar period of the twentieth century drew on representations of indigenous types. There are a number of reasons for this, the main one being no doubt that Africa (apart from Australia, to which I'll briefly return) was the continent – at least in its vast sub-Saharan territories – that had been the most recently colonized by Europe. Its peoples were therefore relatively unknown and their difference – in colour, race and traditions – meant that they were the source of a higher degree of fascination and curiosity. They were of course also ripe for commercial exploitation. In Australia, aborigines had also featured in travel posters (railway as well as airline, see Figures 4.10 and 4.11) and on postage stamps (Figure 4.12) but, owing to their relative (perceived) uniformity, were less subject to exploitation within an exoticizing framework. From the nineteenth century they had also been threatened by

Figure 4.9a Air France Afrique, Jacques Nathan-Garamond, 1960

Figure 4.9b République de Haute Volta 1960, design/engraving René Cottet

the arrival of European settlers more systematically and lethally than the altogether more numerous and various African tribes. So, in posters such as BOAC/Qantas 'Speedbird routes across the world' of 1946 (Figure 3.5) and 'Fly to Australia by BOAC' of 1950 (Figure 3.3), it is the white male Australian settler and not the aborigine who plays the role of welcoming native to the European visitor.

In the Far East, it is noticeable that oriental 'types' are rarely focused on individually but rather shown as a mass (as in the BOAC poster 'Fly to the Far East', Figure 3.10), with the exception of the oriental woman, who, in the case of the Japanese geisha in particular, is presented as an object of erotic,

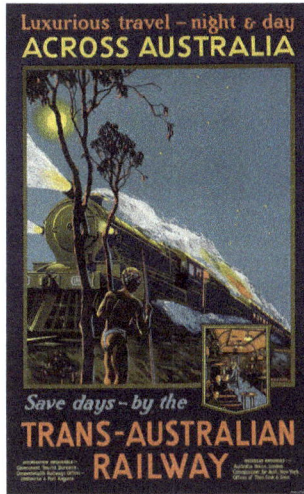

Figure 4.10 Save days by the Trans-Australian Railway, Percival Trompf, 1935

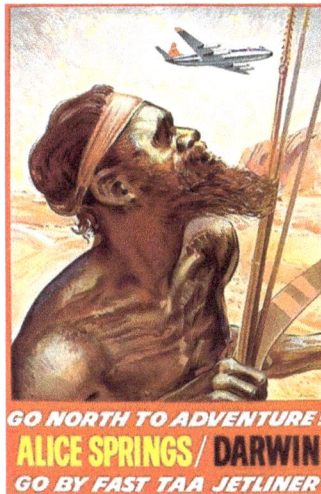

Figure 4.11 Go North to adventure! Go by fast TAA jetliner, Henry Jolles, c. 1960

Figure 4.12 Australian definitive stamp 1950, design Frank D. Manley (based on photo of Gwoya Tjungurrayi by Roy Dunston, 1935)

as well as more generally exotic, fascination – as in the Swissair Japan poster of 1963 (Figure 2.39). Both North and South America, also relatively recently colonized, exploited and then 'granted' independence by European powers, had had their indigenous populations far more drastically marginalized – when they were not simply exterminated – leaving a majority population that was much more of a melting pot or racial 'brassage' of European and some native types than was the case with Africa.

Chapter 5

GLAMOUR AND SEX APPEAL: DESIGNING DESIRE

If as Oscar Wilde asserted 'Dandyism is the assertion of the absolute modernity of beauty', then glamour may be similarly defined in relation to feminine attractiveness. As a term, glamour began to be widely used after World War I with the rise of Hollywood cinema and still photography, and it implies a certain element of contemporaneous artificiality: make-up, hair styling, grooming, fashionable clothes are all important elements of glamorization. Although male film stars were submitted to a grooming almost as thorough as Hollywood goddesses, glamour nevertheless remains a primarily feminine attribute, although it can with a provocative edge also be applied to men, especially those who find themselves in the limelight of celebrity in sport or the entertainment business. Men in the public eye, like men in military uniform ready for inspection, have always been expected to look smart. When, in the twentieth century, women started wearing military uniforms (which apart from the substitution of skirts for trousers more or less followed the standard male pattern), masculine smartness became a prerequisite aimed in part at somewhat toning down feminine attractiveness. So early airline hostess outfits, when they were not, as they were in American airlines of the 1930s, modelled on nurses' uniforms, exhibited a certain masculine severity (Figure 5.1) that was, however, softened by the pretty, discreetly made-up, feminine face.

The contrast between masculine uniform and feminine attractiveness is perfectly allegorized in an Ansett poster of c. 1960 (Figure 5.2) in which a pretty, blond, blue-eyed airhostess stands next to a stereotypically tall and handsome airline pilot. The pilot wears the dark uniform (emblazoned with medal stripes as well as wings), the white-topped cap and spotless white shirt and black tie of a naval captain. The hostess wears an outfit that is a kind of parody of a uniform in which the soft grey-green serge of the cap and jacket is set off by an open-collared off-white blouse (the tie was omitted from most airhostesses' uniforms from c. 1950). The pilot's direct gaze and firm facial expression contrast with the hostess's soft blue eyes and broader smile. He represents masculine capability and assurance, steadiness and maturity of judgement;

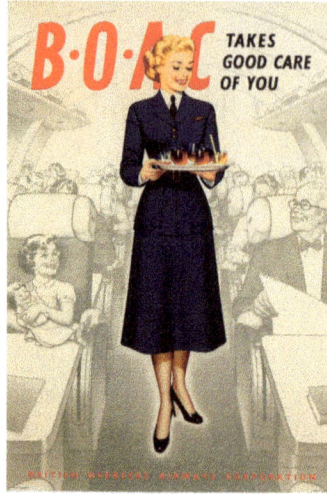

Figure 5.1 BOAC takes good care of you, late 1940s

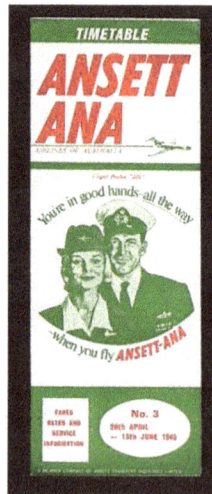

Figure 5.2 ANSETT ANA You're in good hands – all the way, c. 1960

she stands for feminine attentiveness and sexual attraction, the jingle accompanying the poster image 'You're in good hands – All the way – When you fly Ansett – ANA' possibly playing on the ambivalence of the phrases 'in good hands' and 'All the way'.

Figure 5.3 Fly Swissair, Hans Looser, 1955

The sexual allure of this tension between masculine uniform and feminine attractiveness was soon recognized by the major international airlines, in particular in the fashion-conscious 1950s, with the result that the airhostess or air stewardess becomes increasingly an object of fantasy identification as well as a provider of reassurance and comfort to airline travellers. She is correspondingly exhibited in this role in an increasing number of airline posters in the post-World War II period. Like the 'glamour destination' discussed in Chapter 2, the airhostess becomes a focus of desire, the promise of which, although not necessarily fulfilled in reality, nevertheless has a powerful motivating impact on the airline passenger, particularly if he is a heterosexual male, accompanied or not by his wife (Figure 5.3).

Commercial flying began as a male domain. In the 1920s, most airline income came from the delivery of mail that, being light, made it more profitable to transport post than people. Passengers on routes to remote destinations, especially in Canada and Australia, often had to sit on mailbags, as the mail underwrote the trip. As demand from potential passengers increased, and as aircraft were quicker than ships and could land in places that railways did not reach, fledgling airline companies began to reflect on how to service passenger needs in the sky. Some early posters compared aircraft to express trains (see Figure 3.34), which had long offered dining cars and attentive stewards. In the 1930s, few airlines employed air hostesses, though there were some exceptions (Hudson & Pettifer, 1979: 91).

The first air passengers included the rich and the upper class, an early version of that smart social group that from the 1960s became known as the international jet set, whose members in the 1920s included royalty and bankers. British, French and German companies deliberately courted this market. The first issue of the German periodical *Die Luftreise* outlined those whom it considered suitable passengers; the list included businessmen, tourists, honeymoon couples, directors, lawyers, mannequins, not to mention fresh oysters and crabs, expensive silks and perfumes, and such fragile merchandise as electric bulbs, furs and chemicals.

The *Imperial Airways Monthly Bulletin* boasted of its distinguished and interesting passengers, who on London to Paris services in March 1927 included the Baron de Rothschild; René Clair, the French film producer; Prince and Princess Wolkonsky; and Lord Londonderry, secretary of state for Air. Despite such exalted patronage, businessmen made up the bulk of passengers in the 1920s and 1930s, whether going from capital to capital in Europe, travelling Pan American from continental US to Hawaii, or flying Qantas from Longreach to Brisbane. Wealthy farmers were not uncommon passengers on the latter route (Davidson & Spearritt, 2010: chapter 10).

Although Britain, Germany and France had pioneered air travel in the early 1920s, they were overtaken by the United States later in the decade, though most flights in the United States were internal or to islands in the Pacific. By 1929 the top eight countries (with numbers travelling in parenthesis) in air travel were: United States (162,000), Germany (120,000), Canada (95,000), Australia (80,000), United Kingdom (29,000), France (25,000), Italy (24,000) and the Netherlands (15,000) (Mance, 1943). Passenger numbers fell sharply in the great depression and did not recover until the late 1930s.

As passenger demand grew, larger aircraft were brought into service and male stewards attended to passengers' needs (Hudson & Pettifer, 1979). Many airline job functions adopted the nomenclature of ships' crews, including stewards, pilots and even ship's captain. A young male flight attendant helps the female passenger on board a Lufthansa flight in 1928 (Figure 5.4) while in Dransy's Air France poster of 1933, it is a smiling captain, dressed in white with arms outstretched, who upholds both the map of France and an air-craft. It has long been the pilot's role to assure passengers that they were in good hands.

Women appear early in the role of both passengers and well-wishers in air-line posters, from Japan to Europe. As we saw, in a 1938 Empire Flying Boat poster, immaculately dressed gentlemen and ladies, and a smartly clothed young girl, enjoy the promenade deck while a male steward waits with drinks in the background (Figure 3.20). In a poster of 1946 showing the cross-section of a Short Sandringham flying boat, the captain, first officer and radio officer, all

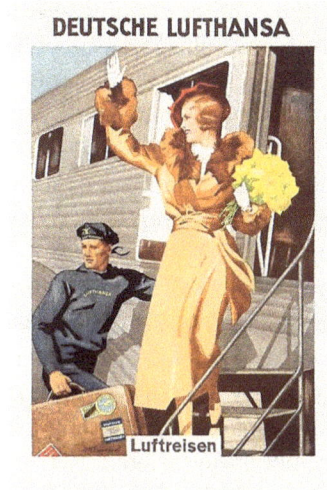

Figure 5.4 Deutsche Lufthansa Luftreisen, Julius U. Engelhard, 1935

men, are in the cockpit, a male steward waits on passengers in the cabin. The aircraft provided separate powder rooms for men and women (Figure 2.17).

One of the challenges facing airlines in the 1930s was that of responding to the expectations of passengers who were regular users of express trains and many of whom regularly crossed the Atlantic on board the great transatlantic liners. On both trains and ships, first-class travellers expected a high standard of comfort. It is more difficult to provide the same comfort on a smaller aircraft, but with the introduction in the 1930s of Fokker tri-motor aircraft by KLM, and larger flying boats by Imperial Airways and Pan Am, passengers were given a high standard of service. Airhostesses were first employed by Boeing in 1930, but when the US government legislated against aircraft manufacturers operating airlines, hostesses came under the United Airlines flag. Trans World Airlines (TWA) launched the world's first hostess academy in 1933, having employed them since 1930 (Hudson & Pettifer, 1979: 91). The initial eight hostesses were registered nurses and wore white uniforms during flight. The Douglas DC3 aircraft they flew in were unheated, cruised at 2000 feet and occasionally had to land in a field to wait for a storm to pass. Swissair and KLM employed their first airhostesses from 1934 and 1935, respectively (Hudson & Pettifer, 1979: 91), with Holyman Airways in Australia following in 1936 and Lufthansa in 1938. KLM promptly withdrew their airhostesses, however, since the young ladies got so many proposals for marriage that they only stayed for a few months of their contract (Hudson & Pettifer, 1979: 91). Holyman Airways hostesses (McRobbie, 1992: 13–22) were not allowed to smoke or drink in public and, with no training, were obliged to school themselves in the psychology of air travel. Hostesses, obliged to retire at 35 years, were not allowed to accept tips and had to be moderate in their use of lipstick and cosmetics. They also had to warn passengers of the risks of walking near propellers while the aircraft was on the ground.

Lufthansa sought ladies of education and breeding (Hudson & Pettifer, 1979: 91), with the ability to give the aircraft cabin a homely, domestic atmosphere (see Figure 1.6). Imperial Airways did not want 'stewardesses' at all, nor did they want a hybrid nurse/waitress on board. They employed white, British flying stewards who could serve six courses, with wines, to between 30 and 40 people in an hour. Imperial Airways remained wedded to the tradition of the great British shipping lines, where male stewards were ubiquitous (Figures 3.14, 3.15 and 3.20), but unlike those employed by Imperial Airways, the stewards on ships were not always white.

Imperial Airways (or, after 1939, BOAC), after World War II, had to abandon its policy of all-male cabin crew, reflecting the dramatic movement of women into the workforce during the war. A BOAC poster from the late 1940s showed a cool, calm and sedately dressed hostess attending to passengers' needs. With the demeanour of a nurse and dressed in shoes, stockings and tie, she might have walked off an RAF base (Figure 5.1). But by the early 1950s BOAC were already emphasizing the sex appeal of their airhostesses: although she still 'takes good care of you', the attention has shifted from her uniform to her smiling face and her attractive figure (Figure 5.5); by 1964, BOAC were employing 734 air stewardesses. From the late 1940s, Pan Am in their posters featuring air hostesses, particularly those advertising the New York–Paris route, were also focusing on their faces, which, attractively made-up, increasingly resembled those of Hollywood stars (Figures 5.6 and 5.7). Joop van Heusden produced a similar image for a KLM poster of 1948 (Figure 5.8) in which the smiling airhostess, whose hairstyle is the same as that of the Pan Am stewardess, serves up New York on a plate to the prospective passenger. A Trans Australia Airlines poster used between 1954 and 1958 combines the British and American approach. It shows Nola Rose, the Bondi Beach bathing beauty contest winner of 1946, as an airhostess, whose blue eyes match the ribbons on the epaulettes of her uniform. But unlike those of the hostesses in most American airline posters, and in those produced a little later by Air France, the TAA hostess's lips are politely sealed, but with an expression that was still friendly (Figure 5.9).

No airline devoted greater care and attention to the role of airhostesses in enhancing the comfort and appeal of their services than the Royal Dutch Airline, KLM. As with other major world airlines, the KLM focus on the airhostess dated from the period after World War II. So, a poster of 1946

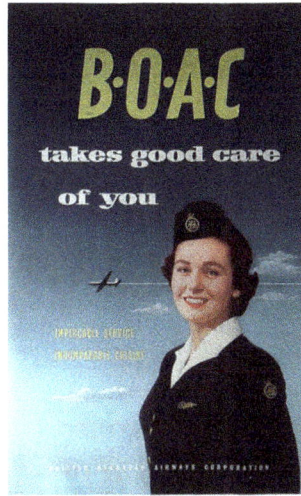

Figure 5.5 BOAC takes good care of you, 1954

Figure 5.6 Pan American, late 1940s

shows a flying Dutch clog, manned by two pilots in which a cosmopolitan mix-
ture of different nationalities is presided over by a smartly dressed airhostess
(Figure 5.10), while in a poster of 1951, the smiling KLM flight crew, including
steward and airhostess, are glimpsed through a porthole as they are about to
board the aircraft. From 1954, KLM produced a series of posters affirming the

Figure 5.7 Enfin! Service direct de Paris à New York Pan American World Airways, late 1940s

Figure 5.8 KLM Serving New York, Joop van Heusden, 1948

Figure 5.9 Fly TAA the friendly way (Nola Rose), 1954

Figure 5.10 KLM Die Vliegende Hollander (flying clog), W. Mahrer, 1946

charms of their female cabin staff on all their major overseas routes – South East Asia, South America and Africa – with a particular emphasis on the female staff members' eyes which, in one poster, are shown seductively gazing at a potential passenger above a Far-Eastern route map (Figure 5.11). In a KLM magazine ad of 1956, a couple happily ensconced in their reclining seats are served by male and female flight staff engaged in numerous different activities to promote their comfort – drawing the porthole curtain, tucking in the blanket, plumping the pillow, pouring the wine and delivering food and refreshments of various sorts. With the jet age of the 1960s, the smiling KLM airhostess, in her simplified but still smart uniform, is juxtaposed with the aircraft's powerful jet engine (Figure 5.12), while in the 1970s the airhostess's many helpful interactions with passengers of all ages and both genders is systematically explored in a series of advertisements promoting the KLM 'Fly the Difference' theme. In this way the mid-1960s slogan 'KLM is often accused of inventing the stewardess' (Figure 5.12) merely confirms the airline's perennial focus on its airhostess cabin service as central to its adver-tising strategy.

The importance of fashion as an aspect of glamour appeal was also not lost on the major world airlines that, from the later 1950s, were regularly updating the uniforms of their air hostesses in the light of clothing trends. Since smartness for men is and always has been fundamentally a function of a well-cut uniform or suit and a neat haircut, little of significance changed in the attire of male air staff. This point is made clear as recently as 2005 in

Figure 5.11 KLM Nach Fernost, Frans Mettes, 1954

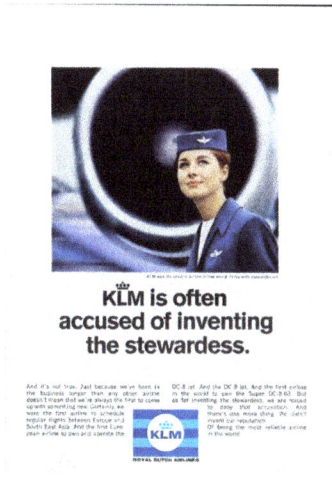

Figure 5.12 'KLM is often accused of inventing the stewardess', Smit's International Advertising, 1965–66

an Air France poster showing Christian Lacroix's new uniform designs for both male and female cabin staff employed by Air France (Figure 5.13). For women, however, the raising or lowering of a hemline, the shaping of a hat or the changing of hairstyles was always a major preoccupation, and this was

Figure 5.13 Air France Nouveaux Uniformes Christian Lacroix, 2005

reflected in airline posters. As one would expect given Paris's prestige, along with London and New York, as a major fashion capital, Air France were particularly attentive in their posters to promote French glamour in the form of its hostesses and their uniforms.

Two Air France posters from the late 1960s and early 1970s reflect the changing image of women as objects of desire. In the 1966 poster (Figure 5.14), the attractive smiling hostess wears her hair long in a style that would have been inconceivable a decade earlier and that looks touchingly absurd beneath the still more or less military-style cap she is wearing. The 1971 poster (Figure 5.15), on the other hand, shows a more demure figure, with neater, shorter, darker hair, adapted better to the peaked cap that is nevertheless worn in a slightly jaunty manner. The hostess's hand is still gloved – gloves as a sign of female smartness had largely disappeared from street fashion in the 1960s though they remain part of airhostess uniforms into the twenty-first century (Figure 5.13) – and her smile is less pronounced than that of the 1960s hostess. The return to relative demureness of attire as witnessed in the 1970s poster may be a reflection of a more general post-1960s awareness that, if the erotic tension between female attractiveness and quasi-military uniform was to be maintained, the two components should be presented in roughly equal balance, one that is clearly in evidence in the 1971 poster. Although Britney Spears in 2003 used the airhostess persona in a typically provocative video to promote herself as the ultimate contemporary object of male fantasy desire, this outrageous presentation would clearly be inappropriate on an

Figure 5.14 Air France (hostess), 1966

Figure 5.15 Air France (hostess), 1971

airline poster in the politically correct world of today's mass, mixed-race and mixed-gender travel.

As competition between airlines increased, so did the pressure to employ hostesses from a variety of ethnic backgrounds. While posters continued to celebrate their glamour, one of the practical reasons for this staffing policy was the need to make a range of languages available to the passengers. A BOAC poster from the late 1950s, aimed at both English- and French-speaking market, showed four hostesses in different styles of uniform (Figure 5.16), implying that while catering for different languages and cultures, the airlines' hostesses could all speak the lingua franca. Smaller regional and cut-price airlines, however, were less concerned with the language ability of their hostesses than with their looks and their figure. Pacific Southwest Airlines posters depicted hostesses dressed like dolly birds in short skirts, posing by the aircraft's tail.

As we saw in Chapter 2, some early posters emphasized the sex appeal of travel not by focusing on the hostesses, who, employed only by some airlines, were rare in the 1930s, but on the exotic female imagined to be awaiting the Western male at his far-flung destination (see Figure 2.35). This tendency is in evidence in many posters of subsequent decades. So, for example, a Swissair poster of 1963 promises the visitor to Japan the chance of meeting a geisha girl (Figure 2.39), as did an Air France poster of the same period advertising the Paris–Tokyo route. As we also saw in Chapter 2, Western Airlines enticed domestic passengers travelling to New York with posters showing dancing girls, frowned over by the Statue of Liberty (Figure 2.44). By the 1960s most airlines promoting travel to famous beach resorts – from Miami and the Bahamas to South America, Australia and continental Europe – lured potential passengers with girls in swimsuits (Figure 2.42). The fantasy of the exotic female was in particular stimulated from the 1960s by Far Eastern airlines – most notably Thai and Singapore – that promoted the oriental good looks of their hostesses as well as their attentive approach to passengers (in particular male ones).

Unsurprisingly, given the advertising function of the poster, graphic designers were not commissioned to depict air or cabin crew attending to emergencies, whether a near-miss between aircraft or a spilt cup of tea. Nor were future passengers to be shown crewmembers dealing with drunken or badly behaved passengers, especially sportsmen returning home in a celebratory mood after a win. Such events are not beyond the artistic repertory of poster designers, but they are more the preserve of the cartoonist and of the send-up movie, as in the film *Flying High* (1980), first entitled *Airplane*, that parodied the already established air disaster movie genre. In this film, a mysterious virus incapacitates the crew and it is only a World War II pilot who, despite a long-held fear of flying, is able to safely land the aircraft.

This film drew macabre inspiration – especially the scenes of confusion in the cockpit – from the world's worst airline disaster. In March 1977 a KLM 747 ploughed into a Pan Am 747 while desperately trying to take off from Tenerife airport. The pilot of the KLM aircraft, Jacob Van Zanten, had been the epitome of the 'you're in safe hands' tradition and had been featured in KLM advertisements and posters. A KLM ad of 1976 showed him in charge

Figure 5.16 All over the world BOAC takes good care of you, A. Cessel, 1959

with the tag line 'from the people who made punctuality possible'. The subsequent investigation into the Tenerife disaster showed that the stereotypically strong male pilot of the KLM craft had a dangerous streak of impatience and a preoccupation with punctuality, the primary cause of the disaster. All crew and passengers on the KLM aircraft died though there were some survivors among crew and passengers on the Pan Am jumbo jet.

Since that accident, pilots have not often featured in airline posters, not least because in the event of a crash they are often held accountable, in a way that is much less likely for other aircrew, or ground crew. The 'black box flight recorder', invented in Australia in the 1950s, to record cockpit and cockpit-to-ground-control conversations, made it much easier for air traffic investigators to assess whether pilot error had contributed to an accident. In the tradition of the ship's captain, the pilot is in control of the vessel and its fate is in his hands.

Those aspects of the operation of airlines that could not be regarded as glamorous, for obvious reasons, do not figure in posters. Servicing, refuelling and engineering checks are vital but assumed parts of the operation. The function of the advertising poster can only ever be to promote good news. On the other hand, posters promoting left-wing attacks on poverty, the ruling class, war and racism could not be characterized as committed to expressing this. It is for this reason that the more utilitarian operations of the airline industry, whether maintenance, the removal of ice from aircraft wings, the loading and unloading of baggage, or the removal of the passenger who died in flight, do not form part of the poster designer's brief.

Poster designers and their airline employers – in practice, usually the head of public relations – have also been traditionally disinclined to focus on points of embarkation, particularly within the airline terminal. This preserve is in any case that of the airport authority rather than the individual airline that merely pays for and uses the airport facility. Until the 1950s most terminals – with the exception of Idlewild and Schiphol – were makeshift, some of them (like the early Heathrow in London) being recently converted from military bases. The point of embarkation is also the primary point of hassle and delay in air travel. The terminal is where it is discovered whether the scheduled flight is late or not, or whether it has been cancelled. Before the widespread use of the internet and the mobile phone, most people did not discover whether their flight would depart on time until they presented themselves at the air terminal. However, even telephoning beforehand was no guarantee in large cities where passengers often left home two or three hours before their scheduled departure time.

No airline poster designer would ever be asked to illustrate the chaos at major airports caused by bad weather, cancelled flights, the failure of ticketing and baggage systems – potentially more drastic now that they are computerized – nor the inordinate delays that anti-terrorist scanning devices inflict on users in all major airports. This is simply not the stuff of posters. In 2010 a controversy erupted over scanning machines in US airports where security staff could in effect view passengers' bodies. No matter how vain an individual might be of their physique, no one claimed this to be a glamorous procedure. In an epoch of mass travel in gigantic airports and super-large aircraft, no matter how comfortable the seats, how delicious the meal or how good the in-flight entertainment, the glamour of airline travel seems increasingly to be a thing of the past.

CONCLUSION: THE DECLINE OF THE AIRLINE TRAVEL POSTER

As was noted in the introduction, the advent of modern colour photography and mass televisual information coincided with both the decline of the airline poster and the increased democratization of airline travel: the jet age and intense commercial competition have ushered in a very different approach to airline promotion from that of the pre-1960s. In the modern period air travel has become banal, a mass phenomenon, intrinsic to the global expansion of tourism as well as business; as Hudson and Pettifer confirm, for every one passenger in 1939, there were 1000 in 1979 (1979: 90). As a result, the images used to promote it draw increasingly on a standardized, internationalist repertory that one might find in any glossy magazine or journal and so lose much of the specific flavour and charm evident in posters produced for public display in a less democratic and homogeneous era. In an age when the concept of exoticism has become problematic – the modern air traveller being as likely as not to be him- or herself previously categorized as 'exotic' (i.e. non-Western) – it becomes increasingly difficult to romanticize travel destinations. The skyline and airport at the many scheduled points of arrival or departure are furthermore becoming more difficult to distinguish from each other. This is in particular true of the airport itself which is now generally recognized as being a *non-lieu* or non-place, that is, a site lacking in historical, cultural or individual significance: it is a place of banality, boredom and delay. The aircraft has in a similar way become emptied of individual character: all models, whether manufactured by Airbus or by Boeing, are virtually identical in appearance and are indeed very often not seen from the outside at all by their passengers who board them along a covered gangway. Plane-spotting, like trainspotting, has become a thing of the past. The focus on destination in its larger sense rather than itinerary has further reduced the imaginative appeal of travel and its scope for representation.

The text of *Design in Airline Travel Posters* opened with a comparison of two posters from two very different ages of airline travel, one from 1959 (a moment close to the chronological limit of this study) and one of 1990. By way of conclusion, a second look at these two advertisements tells much about the decline in style and persuasiveness of airline travel posters from the 1960s onwards and the changes in both the conception and experience of travel in the later jet age.

First let us briefly summarize the formal and media-related differences between the two images: the 1959 BOAC poster (Figure 1.2) is a colour lithograph, while that of the 1990 Australian Airlines (Figure 1.1) is a juxtaposition of two colour photographs: one fully integrates text and image, the other superimposes text on image or marginalizes text in relation to image; one places the name of airline and destination centrally, the other situates these components at the margins; one crops the principal, dynamic figure in such a way as to lead it out and towards the viewer, the other leads the viewer *into* the image in a voyeuristic trajectory towards the group of naked figures in the centre; one expresses the erotic appeal of the destination in a public, festive and exuberant way, the other invites the viewer to intrude on the (supposed) privacy of three naked and intertwined figures in a manner that is voyeuristic, if not pornographic.

The above – admittedly somewhat schematic – summary points to a more general and essential difference between pre-1970 and post-1970 airline travel poster design: the former's mastery of the medium and technique of graphic art as opposed to the relatively simplistic composition of the latter, drawing principally on photography. The former's mastery is based principally on the selection, editing and coordination of visual (which includes textual) information, leading to an overall effect of pictorial integrity, a visual rhetoric of persuasion. So, in the *BOAC South America* poster, the woman, the décor of festivity and the key (but minimalist) textual information (in particular the famous BOAC logo) all surge into our awareness against the pregnant darkness of the unified backdrop. The individual components of the ensemble have been carefully selected and edited, juxtaposed to promote maximum legibility and aesthetic effect, a strategy that colour lithography uniquely facilitates. This is because the imaginative links between the words and images presented have been internalized and then re-presented as part of the artistic process so that the final imaginative vision is easily shared with, processed and enjoyed by the viewer.

By contrast, the 1990 Australian Airlines poster proposes a muddled and disconcerting image. The reasons for this are largely a function of failure in selection, editing and coordination of the visual and textual components. In the first place, the textual elements hardly assert themselves as being in any way *visually* persuasive: they are purely *anchors* (to use Roland Barthes's terms, 1964: 40–51) that situate the two images and attempt to bring them into close *rapport*. They provide pure information; they add little to the glamour or logic of the pictorial components of the design. Second, as was shown in Chapter 1, the juxtaposition of the two colour photos that constitute the main image seems arbitrary and unpersuasive: the banal, real-estate brochure photo of the Gold Coast shoreline is hardly related to the erotic scenario enacted on what is presumably the balcony of one of the resort's high-rise apartment blocks. The modern traveller and the modern viewer, it implies, are not interested in the imaginative or cultural ethos of the place, but merely the possibility of fulfilling there an individual fantasy that could be enacted in any modern seaside city on the globe. The photogenic nakedness of the three bodies, in its precise and clinical arrangement, attests to a failure of rather than a stimulus to the viewer's imagination, offering, like pornography, possible immediate sexual gratification but no deeper meaning. The still-life of Egyptian objects in the bottom right-hand corner furthermore furnishes very little by way of mythical alibi.

Airline travel has in the late modern era lost much of the glamour and excitement attached to it in the pre-1960s. It has become an integral part of modern life, merging seamlessly with work, pleasure or other habitual activities. Most of today's journeys, whether for holiday or business, are identified and booked online. With the radical widening of consumer choice and commercial competitiveness, choice of destination or itinerary has become a largely economic issue. The world has, since the pioneering air travel days of the 1930s and 1940s, become so small that its individual parts have lost much of their aura of difference or fascination, the destination asserting itself (even for holidays) as a primarily functional choice. Even so-called glamour destinations – the major capitals of the world, the major beach resorts, the major historical or cultural sites – are in the internet age now so easily accessible that there is little need to link their attractions to the mode of travel to them.

Since late modern airline travel bears little trace of myth or romance, so the posters that promote it have become similarly lacking in imaginative appeal. It is with a renewed sense of interest as well as of nostalgia, therefore, that cultural historians and collectors turn to explore the early age of airline travel and the advertisements promoting it. It has in itself become something of a foreign country, opening up half-forgotten tracks into exotic worlds in which the unknown and the different still offer an imaginative challenge and provide a sense of strangeness or adventure. In this way, the *signs* of travel in that past era still carry the sensuous fascination of the signifier, leading to a reverie and reflection mostly absent from contemporary travel posters.

REFERENCES

Barthes, Roland (1964) 'Rhétorique de l'image', *Communications*, 4 (1964), 40–51.

Castiglioni, Luigi (1986) *Le Sport en affiches*, Paris: Editions alternatives.

Cruddas, Colin (2008) *100 Years of Advertising in British Aviation*, Stroud: History Press.

Davidson, Jim and Spearritt, Peter (2010) *Holiday Business: Tourism in Australia since 1870* (chapter 10, Air travel and the rise of the resort), Melbourne: Melbourne University Press.

Durry, Jean (1988) *Le Sport à l'affiche*, Paris: Hoëbeke.

Franciscono, Marcel (1987) *The Modern Dutch Poster. The First Fifty Years 1890–1940*, Cambridge, MA: MIT Press.

Fresnault-Deruelle, Pierre (1989) *Les Images prises aux mots: rhétorique de l'image fixe*, Paris: Edligi.

——— (1997) *L'Image placardée. Pragmatique et rhétorique de l'affiche* Paris: Nathan.

Gervereau, Laurent (1991) *La Propagande par l'affiche*, Paris: Syros-Alternatives.

——— (2000) *Les Images qui mentent. Histoire du visuel au XXe siècle*, Paris: Editions du Seuil.

Guillemain, Alain (1991) *La Politique s'affiche. Les affiches de la politique*, Paris: Didier Erudition/Presses Universitaires de Provence.

Hudson, Kenneth and Pettifer, Julian (1979) *Diamonds in the Sky: A Social History of Air Travel*, London: Bodley Head.

Mance, Sir Harry Osborne (1943) *International Air Transport*, London: Oxford University Press.

McRobbie, Margaret (1992) *Walking the Skies: The First Fifty Years of Air Hostessing in Australia 1936–1986*, self-published, Melbourne, 13–22.

Moles, Abraham A. (1970) *L'Affiche dans la société urbaine*, Paris: Dunod.

Morris, Jan (1989) *Riding the Skies. Classic Posters from the Golden Age of Flying*, London: Bloomsbury.

Müller-Brockman, Josef and Yoshikawa, Shizuko (1971) *History of the Poster*, Zürich: ABC Verlag.

Peignot, Jérôme (1988) *Air France: Affiches, Posters 1933–1983*, Paris: Hazan.

Purvis, Alston W. (1992) *Dutch Graphic Design, 1918–1945*, New York: Van Nostrand Reinhold.

Said, Edward (1979) *Orientalism*, London: Routledge.

Scott, David (1995) *European Stamp Design. A Semiotic Approach*, London: Academy Editions.

——— (2002) 'L'image ethnographique: le timbre-poste colonial français de 1920 à 1950', *Protée*, 30 no. 2 (2002), 45–54.

——— (2010) *Poetics of the Poster. The Rhetoric of Image/Text*, Liverpool: Liverpool University Press.

——— (2020) 'Post and the Postage Stamp as (Post-)colonial *Place of Memory*', in *Postcolonial Realms of Memory* (ed. Etienne Achille, Charles Forsdick and Lydie Moudelino), Liverpool: Liverpool University Press, 351–59.

Scudiero, Maurizio, Cirulli, Massimo and Cremoncini, Roberta (2002) *Planespotting: Italian Aviation Posters 1910–1943*, New York: Publicity Press.

Smit, G. I., Wunderlinck, R. C. J. and Hooland, I. (1994) *KLM in Beeld. 75 jaar vormgeving en promotie*, Naarden: V&K.

Spearritt, Peter (1990) *Trading Places. Australian Travel Posters 1909–1990*, Monash University Gallery/National Centre for Australian Studies.

Weill, Alain (1994) *L'Invitation au voyage. L'affiche de tourisme dans le monde*, Paris: Somogy.

Woodley, Charles (2004) *BOAC. An Illustrated History*, Stroud: Tempus.

INDEX

Note: Page references in romans. *Figure (Illustration) numbers in italics.*

www.ingramcontent.com/pod-product-compliance
Lightning Source LLC
Chambersburg PA
CBHW071134280326
41935CB00010B/1217